AF841453

ROUTLEDGE LIBRARY EDITIONS:
RESPONDING TO FASCISM

THE NAZI DICTATORSHIP

THE NAZI DICTATORSHIP

ROY PASCAL

Volume 3

Routledge
Taylor & Francis Group
LONDON AND NEW YORK

First published in English 1934

This edition first published in 2010
by Routledge
2 Park Square, Milton Park, Abingdon, Oxon, OX14 4RN

Simultaneously published in the USA and Canada
by Routledge
270 Madison Avenue, New York, NY 10016

Routledge is an imprint of the Taylor & Francis Group, an informa business

© 1934 Roy Pascal

All rights reserved. No part of this book may be reprinted or reproduced or utilised in any form or by any electronic, mechanical, or other means, now known or hereafter invented, including photocopying and recording, or in any information storage or retrieval system, without permission in writing from the publishers.

British Library Cataloguing in Publication Data
A catalogue record for this book is available from the British Library

ISBN 10: 0-415-57699-7 (Set)
eISBN 10: 0-203-85012-2 (Set)
ISBN 10: 0-415-58078-1 (Volume 3)
eISBN 10: 0-203-85022-X (Volume 3)

ISBN 13: 978-0-415-57699-4 (Set)
eISBN 13: 978-0-203-85012-1 (Set)
ISBN 13: 978-0-415-58078-6 (Volume 3)
eISBN 13: 978-0-203-85022-0 (Volume 3)

Publisher's Note
The publisher has gone to great lengths to ensure the quality of this reprint but points out that some imperfections in the original copies may be apparent.

Disclaimer
The publisher has made every effort to trace copyright holders and would welcome correspondence from those they have been unable to trace.

THE NAZI DICTATORSHIP

By
ROY PASCAL

LONDON
GEORGE ROUTLEDGE & SONS, LTD.
BROADWAY HOUSE: 68–74 CARTER LANE, E.C.
1934

Printed in Great Britain by Butler & Tanner Ltd., Frome and London

CONTENTS

CONTENTS

FOREWORD

AMONG the many books and articles written against Hitler, two conceptions of National-Socialism are dominant. Some hold that it is the recrudescence of the old Imperialistic Barbarism which precipitated the Great War ; some that it is a passing disease, which decent Germans will soon throw off. Threats or blandishments will, it is hoped, shake Germany out of its folly.

In the present book Hitlerism is treated neither as a national German characteristic nor as a passing madness. It has been my aim to trace the conditions which encouraged the expansion of Hitlerism, and the permanent influence that National-Socialism has exerted on German society.

An unambiguous development is clear—particularly clear since Hitler came to power. Germany is now the State of Monopoly-Capitalism, of a Dictatorship, not of a set of gangsters, nor of a political Party, but of the great industrial and financial interests, whose might in the last eighteen months has been vastly strengthened and extended.

It is this State of Monopoly-Capitalism which I have described in the latter half of this book. National-Socialism is the political movement which formed this society. Its future policy, its strength, its mode of expression and action, the possibility of overthrowing Hitlerism, are matters which can be forecast only if this underlying reality is comprehended.

THE NAZI DICTATORSHIP

CHAPTER I

THE GERMAN REVOLUTION OF 1918

In the last days of the reign of William II, when the armies were in full retreat and revolt was sweeping over the land, Max von Baden summoned the Social-Democratic Party to take office. Ebert became the first Social-Democratic Chancellor, as the last rampart of the Monarchy. Immediately after taking office, Scheidemann, the Social-Democratic Minister, addressed the masses outside the *Reichstag*, exhorting them to stabilise the Socialist victory, as if the Revolution were already won. The first manifesto of the new government called on the German People to " leave the streets, preserve peace and quiet ". Relations of confidence were established between the new government and the General Staff. Leaders of industry and representatives of Social-Democracy sat down together to fashion a " Working Association " between capital and labour.

But a real Revolution threatened from underneath. In 1916 the revolutionary Spartacus League had been formed. In 1917 the Independent Socialist Party had arisen out of a split in the Social-Democratic ranks. From this time a wave of working-class action against the War and the War governments, against the policy of collaboration of the Social-Democratic leadership, had slowly mounted in Germany. There had been strikes and food-riots in 1917, culminating in the famous munition-strike of 1918—the "stab in the back". There had been the mutiny in the Fleet in the spring of 1917. In November 1918 occurred the decisive blow, the mutiny at Kiel. The ships of war ran up the red flag, and were in the hands of Sailors' Councils. This was the signal for the Revolution. In factories and in the army Councils of Workers and Soldiers were formed, on the model of the Russian Soviets. The old authorities were thrown out of their offices and stripped of power. On the basis of these Councils a new constitution was to be given to Germany, a Socialistic Republic was to be created. A great meeting of representatives of the Councils was called to Berlin for December 16, to constitute the new government.

Social-Democracy had quickly recognised where the new centre of power lay. They had thrown off their allegiance to William II, who had abdicated. Noske had been sent to Kiel, where he had been successful in asserting the control of the Social-Democratic Party over the insurgents.[1] Frenzied efforts were made by the Party to win the trust of the Workers' and Soldiers' Councils, to get its nominees sent to the Congress of December 16. The results were of tremendous significance. At the Congress all Parties were agreed that the Councils should form a government of People's Representatives. But while Spartacus and the Independents demanded a govern-

[1] See Noske, *Von Kiel bis Kapp*.

ment of the working-class, the Social-Democrats opposed the idea of a class-dictatorship, and guaranteed, for the time, the security of private property. By virtue of their energetic protestations of their socialist faith, and as a result of their old and powerful organisation, the Social-Democrats won a decisive victory. Ninety-eight representatives voted under the leadership of Luxemburg and Liebknecht for a government of the working-class, 344 put their faith in the democratic tactics of the Social-Democratic Party, who promised socialism if a general election proved it to be the desire of the people. The provisional result was a coalition government of People's Representatives, consisting of three Independents and three Social-Democrats. For the time, the coalition with the Independents gave the Social-Democrats an appearance of radical determination. When the forces of Reaction, the Army, etc. had recovered a little they were able to throw off this alliance and joyfully announce that the Independents had left the Government.

The decisions of the Congress of Workers' and Soldiers' Councils meant the cessation of much of the revolutionary activity. The first Manifesto of this government established certain liberties (of the Press, of Association, etc.) and social reforms such as the eight-hour day. The revolutionary movement had already gone far beyond these measures, and in many places was establishing control by the working-class. The government's chief political task became the "preservation of the Republic", i.e. the countering of this working-class movement. Under Noske's leadership a Citizens' Defence Corps was organised to keep order. In this were absorbed the troops which had remained faithful to the Monarchy, under their old officers—a predominantly aristocratic class—and special troops of Irregulars, Black Hundreds. Among these was a Company under Ernst Röhm, at that time an open enemy of the new Republic, and later the organiser of Hitler's Storm Troops.[1] From this Citizens' Defence Corps was later recruited the Army of the Republic, to be officered by the same set of anti-republican professional soldiers.

For some time Berlin and Dresden and other large cities were in the hands of the Workers' and Soldiers' Councils. But the policy of the Councils was confused, and immense obstacles were put in their path. Spartacus was an organisation of recent origin, and, in spite of its reputation, small—it is reckoned that its membership was never greater than 2,000. The Independents were still unwilling to break with the Social-Democratic Party. The revolutionaries were divided in their allegiance, believing still that the Social-Democrats would lead them to power and socialism. Everywhere there arose bitter struggles between the government of People's Representatives and the Workers' Councils. In Berlin workers' demonstrations were broken up by the police and Citizens' Defence Corps. Liebknecht and Luxemburg were captured and killed by the Defence Corps. Finally the bands of soldiers, organised and barracked by Noske outside Berlin, marched into the city, drove the representatives of the Workers' Councils out of

[1] See Röhm, *Geschichte eines Hochverräters*, 1928.

their headquarters, and left the Social-Democrats —Ebert, Scheidemann, Noske—in charge. Similar tactics were employed in Saxon towns.[1] The Social-Democrats then called elections for a National Constituent Assembly, stating that they repudiated the authority given them by the Congress of Workers' and Soldiers' Councils.

In Bavaria events followed a slightly different course. Here Social-Democracy had always been weaker and could not so easily control the masses. In March 1919 the Bavarian Commune was set up, under Kurt Eisner, to last for three weeks. For this time the working-class had control of the administrative and defence apparatus. But their forces were small, their methods confused, and they were isolated in Munich. When Eisner was killed even greater confusion reigned. Troops of the Republican Army were moved from the Bavarian frontiers to Munich, under the command of Hitler's later patron, General von Epp, and the Commune was crushed with great severity. For many years afterwards a reactionary, anti-democratic government ruled in Bavaria, giving moral and material support to Hitler's young movement.

The Weimar Constitution and Socialism

For the time being, the revolutionary movement was beaten back. The Workers' and Soldiers' Councils were disbanded. But the fire of revolt broke out again and again, in more and more dangerous forms

[1] A moving picture of the events in Saxony has been given by Ludwig Renn in his novel *Nachkrieg*.

since the foundation of the Communist Party on January 1, 1919. Everywhere the influence of the unrest among the working-class population is evident. Even the middle-class political Parties promised socialisation of monopolies, the break-up of the large estates of the Junkers, the legal recognition of the Trade Unions. On all hands promises were made that the workers would be given a share in the control of the Republic. The Constitution was passed while huge strikes in the coal-fields of the Ruhr were raging. Through its concessions to the workers it could justly pride itself on establishing the "freest Republic" in the world.

The Constitution did not give socialism. But it promised the socialisation of all enterprises which were "suitable" for social administration. The government was to take part in the administration of industry. It could force firms to belong to the federation of their industry, and could send representatives to sit on the board of these federations. It made the Trade Unions the legal representatives of the employees, with the right of establishing conditions of labour with the employers. It further created Factory Councils, elected by the workers of each factory over a certain size, through which the workers could vent grievances and exert pressure on the factory management. District Workers' Councils and a National Workers' Council were promised, but were never realised. They had too much the appearance of Soviets.

All these concessions to the proletariat were granted in order to allay its suspicions of the new Republic.

The result was to strengthen the general faith in Social-Democracy, which was by far the biggest Party in the elections of 1919. The Trade Unions, largely under Social-Democratic control, reached the enormous membership of about 8 millions. In January of that year investigatory committees were set up to consider the socialisation of the coalmining and potash industries. At the end of 1919 a law was actually passed preparatory to the socialisation of the electrical industry. But all these measures proved abortive, and led at most to the establishment of employers' federations in these industries, whose decisions were backed by the State.

Disillusionment on the major question of socialism was accompanied by disillusionment on smaller matters. The years between the Revolution and 1924 were marked by a series of bitter strikes, which were aimed directly or indirectly against the Republic and its midwife, the Social-Democratic Party. Wage-agreements were found to be unsatisfactory, or even not observed; in 1924 the coal-owners under the leadership of Stinnes publicly repudiated them. The Factory Councils attempted repeatedly to assert their will over the factory owners, but with less and less success. In 1920 a Communist rising, under Max Hoelz, maintained itself for several weeks in Middle Germany. Again the revolutionary organisation proved itself weak, for the rising remained isolated, and was repudiated even by the Communist leadership of the time. Other armed risings in Hamburg, Saxony and Thuringia suffered the same fate.

The biggest and best-organised attempt to create

a Workers' Republic was carried out in the Ruhr. In January 1919 a general strike was declared, and the socialisation of the mines proclaimed. The workers were armed and took possession of administrative buildings. Again troops sent from Berlin beat back the insurgents. A year later a monarchist coup was carried out, the so-called Kapp Putsch. Kapp found a tacit ally in these same Republican troops. The predominantly Social-Democratic government had to flee, and called on the Red troops it had formerly suppressed to restore the Republic. The general strike, carried out by armed workers, defeated Kapp. But the action in the Ruhr swelled to large dimensions. The armed workers, driving back the reactionaries, made their objective the establishment of a workers' dictatorship. The government they had reinstated now turned on them. The army, which had looked on while Kapp marched into Berlin, now advanced into the Ruhr. The proletarian troops were destroyed. Afterwards Severing, the Prussian Minister of the Interior, a Social-Democrat, put the whole Ruhr under the closest police supervision, clearing it of arms, making impossible any future military action on the part of the workers. The Social-Democratic Prussian government preferred the risk of another reactionary rising to that of a renewed proletarian action.

Till the end of 1924 the Republic was not out of danger. The number of Social-Democratic members of the *Reichstag* dropped from 165 in 1919 to 100 in May 1924; Liberal-Democratic Party dropped from 75 to 28. The Parties of the Right grew, and the

Communist Party increased from 4 members in 1920 to 62 in 1924 (after a fusion with the Independent Socialists). These were the post-War years of crisis, of inflation. The social reforms of the democratic Republic were unavailing here; capitalism was showing that it could produce new and unheard-of distress. The French marched into the Ruhr in the Spring of 1923. The general strike came to nothing, for the government would not trust the workers and arm them. The Republic could not protect its own frontiers, as the Bolsheviks had done during the Intervention. There were two actions taken against the Republic in this year of 1923, which provide us with a curious illustration of the political situation in Germany.

In Saxony in the Summer the Left wing of the Socialist Party was in power. Under the stress of the desperation of the masses they entered into negotiations with the Communist Party to form a Coalition government. As soon as final preparations for a joint government had been made, Ebert, the Social-Democratic President of the *Reich*, ordered the army to march into Saxony. A military dictatorship was installed, and the defence forces of the abortive government broken up. Thus a legally constituted government was deposed by the army acting on the commands of the President. This precedent loomed large in the political view in 1932 and 1933. But we may contrast this action of a Social-Democratic President towards a Socialist government with that of Hindenburg, the President elected by Social-Democratic votes, towards Hitler.

The other significant event of the year was the Hitler *Putsch* in November. High officers of the army and Munich industrialists had built up Hitler's movement and now utilised it to attempt a *coup d'état* in Bavaria. They did not find the expected allies in governmental circles and the insurgents were fired on. Some were captured only to be set free on a parole they abused (Göring). Others were brought to justice and escaped scot-free. Ludendorff was treated respectfully and granted bail. Hitler, for this act of High Treason, was given a year's imprisonment in a fortress, the lightest kind of imprisonment. Most of the army officers incriminated in the rising were not even dismissed the service. This was the Justice of the Republic.

The strength of a State may be measured by the loyalty of the members of its executive and administrative apparatus. We have seen how the *Reichswehr*, the Republican Army, was formed. It was dominated by aristocratic, anti-democratic officers, who at a suitable moment would not scruple to overthrow the government. These men supported, to a considerable extent out of army funds, the illegal bands of Irregulars, who carried out a systematic Terror during the first years of the Republic, and were ultimately absorbed in Hitler's Storm Troops. Hitler himself was at first, still as a member of the army, a liaison officer between the army and a reactionary political Party. Apart from the army, however, the old bureaucracy was maintained under the Republic. All judges and state-lawyers who felt that it went against their conscience to serve under the new masters were summoned by the Republic to resign. One did so. The result was a Justice which became a by-word in the world. Of 12 political murders committed in the first period of the Republic by members of Left Parties, 9 were punished by death; of 314 by members of the Right, none. The murderers of Rathenau and Erzberger remained unscathed. The trials of Nazis and members of other Right organisations, who made no secret of their delight in violent methods, were marked by that bonhomie which is visible also in the few trials of British Fascists.

In the governmental bureaucracy no radical changes were made. The old imperial machine was taken over *en bloc*, and the few modifications were attended by doubtful results. The post of mayor in the larger cities was made a salaried position, thus making it possible for this post to be held by men without private means. Particularly in States which had a constant Social-Democratic government, such as Prussia, the policy of peaceful penetration was adopted. Slowly Social-Democrats were put into post after post, responsible places in administration and police fell into the hands of the Social-Democratic Party. It was stated by the Socialists that this process would bring about a transformation in the bureaucracy. Actually the opposite result was attained. Men joined the Socialists with the hope that a job would follow. A subtle corruption filtered through the Party. True, these Socialist officials were true to the Party, their sponsor. But their loyalty was to the Party apparatus, not to the Socialist principles or the working-class. They became useless in the fight against Reaction, strong in the fight against all attacks directed from the Left against the State. Their aim was to preserve the State as it was, with its thousands of comfortable nests. They wished to make themselves " comfortable within Capitalism ", as it was put. Thus they were ready for the concessions to dictatorship granted by the Social-Democrats to Brüning, and collapsed miserably before Hitler. The bitterest complaint many of them had to make against Hitler was that, after they had lost their good posts, they were not allowed to have their due pension.

The result of the Revolution of 1918 was pitiful for the makers of this Revolution. Social-Democratic spokesmen later indignantly denied that the Social-Democratic Party was responsible for or wanted the Revolution. Its originators were the workers and soldiers, largely in spontaneous revolt against the war-makers. They revolted against all the classes which had combined to wage war, the monarchy, the landed nobility, the capitalists of all sorts. The original form of revolt, the Workers' and Soldiers' Councils were consciously working-class organs, the basis of a socialistic State. What actually settled out of this ferment was the democratic Republic, a capitalist State. The possessing class was still dominant and filled the key positions of the *Reich* with its adherents. The development of the *Reich* was to be fundamentally determined in the future by the necessities of capitalist economy. The law of profit was to be maintained by the whole apparatus of State. The workers' defensive organisations, Factory Councils, Trade Unions, political Parties, were allowed to speak and bargain, but not to control. To this the immense struggles and sacrifice of the Revolution led.

The Failure of the Revolution

We have to ask, To what is it due that the Revolution of 1918 pursued the course it did? Why did Social-Democracy support Democracy against Socialism? Many writers, for purposes of attack or defence, ascribe the responsibility for the events of 1918 and 1919 to subjective forces. The workers and soldiers were " tired ", and wished only to settle down quietly; or, hostile critics of many parties have charged the Social-Democratic leaders with treachery and hypocrisy. But, if subjective elements alone are to be considered, it is impossible to explain why the Revolution in Russia should have taken so different a course. There are deeper-lying causes which reveal themselves in every manifestation of the Revolution of this period.

The prime cause of the defeat of the Socialist Revolution was the whole theory and practice of the Social-Democratic Party. Most startlingly in its support of the German government in the War this Party had shown that it recognised that the interests of the State came before the interests of the working-class, i.e. had shown that it claimed only to represent the interests of a portion of the population of the State, and was not a Revolutionary Party aiming at the overthrow of the whole social order. Tendencies towards this conception of the working-class had existed in the Social-Democratic Party since its inception. Karl Marx, in his *Critique of the Gotha Programme of the Social-Democratic Party* (1875), attacked this very attitude, then only beginning to invadc the policy of the Socialists. He there points out that the fundamental points in the Party Programme might be used by their opponents in the defence of existing social conditions. The vital, conscious abdication of revolutionary principle in the Party came in the 'nineties, when Bismarck's repressive measures had given way to Wilhelm II's more liberal policy. Here Marx's theory of the accumulation of capital and of the increasing impoverishment of the working-classes was argued to be wrong, chiefly under the leadership of E. Bernstein. The concrete result was " Reformism ", the view that the working-class could look forward to an unlimited vista of social reform in the future, within the framework of capitalist society, that the economic system itself could be slowly transformed into a socialistic system by means of the democratic vote.

There is an essential similarity between this " socialism " and that of the Socialist Parties in England and France. It is based on the situation of the working-class in these countries. The German working-class in the twentieth century was beginning to participate in the advantages of capitalistic imperialism. Large-scale exploitation of colonial countries and peoples, the conquest of the export market, fused to some extent the interests of workers and employers. Conditions in the working-class did improve—though the theoreticians who so proudly proclaimed this fact did not reckon in the growth of poverty in the colonial peoples. In spite of this improvement at all Party-congresses the "conciliationists" were defeated by the votes of the mass, who were unable to accept the view that their interests were identical with those of their employers. On the question of war, too, grave weaknesses were revealed. While the whole Party voted at its Congresses against war and saw clearly that the threatening war arose from the clash of imperialist interests, yet the general policy of conciliation bound the Party more and more to the German government. Hence that collapse of German Social-Democracy, of the whole Second International, at the outbreak of the War of 1914, which has stood to its lasting discredit in the eyes of the working-class.

Not all Social-Democrats by any means acquiesced in this devolution of Marxist thought, of revolutionary practice. Some of the leaders—notably Liebknecht—and many of the members opposed tooth and nail the practice of the Party and Trade Unions, which were identified with the conciliatory policy of the Social-Democratic Party. But this divergence of view did not lead, as in Russia, to the formation of a separate, purely Marxist and Revolutionary Party. Liebknecht and Rosa Luxemburg remained within the Social-Democratic Party until after the outbreak of war.[1] As a result there was no organisation, no publicity-organs through which they could build up a revolutionary nucleus round which the Revolution could

[1] When the Social-Democratic Party voted war-credits on August 4, 1914, Liebknecht absented himself from the *Reichstag*. In December of that year he voted alone against further credits.

form, until the Spartacus League was organised. Existing only under war conditions, the Spartacus League could not expand quickly or train a great number of revolutionary leaders. Lacking the prestige and experience of long years of revolutionary practice, of working-class leadership, it could not take the lead during the vital days of the Revolution, in November and December 1918. The masses, accustomed to look to the Social-Democratic and Trade Union leadership for guidance, still did not abandon it at the time of the Revolution. They felt the slogan of the " Dictatorship of the proletariat ", and the organisational form of Workers' and Soldiers' Councils, to be alien to them. Long before 1918 the Social-Democratic Party was welded to the capitalist State ; and only shortly before the Revolution was a purely working-class, Revolutionary Party formed. To these two facts is due the failure of the Revolution of 1918 to be a Socialist Revolution.

CHAPTER II

THE WEIMAR REPUBLIC

THE Weimar Republic was established by the Social-Democratic Party as a progressive democracy which would inevitably lead to socialism. The principle of majority-rule was accepted as definitive, to be realised in a parliament elected by universal suffrage. In 1919 there were 23,400,000 Germans who voted for democracy, against 4,700,000 opponents from the Right and 2,300,000 from the Left. In November 1932, the last free election in Germany, 13 millions voted for the Republic, against 21,300,000 (15 millions from the Right and 6 millions from the Left). It is now said in Germany that the Germans had no inherent love for democracy and that the 1932 vote represents their true attitude; learned professors have shown that since the time of Tacitus the Germans have only desired a Leader to take their responsibilities out of their hands. But this is an argument in a vicious circle. We have to weigh up what real meaning underlies this phrase, for or against democracy. What liberty to the individual did democracy ensure? What experiences have led the German people to abandon democracy, in favour of what?

The dominant impression carried away by the visitor to Germany in the period of the Republic was that of the freest and most radical culture in the whole of the capitalist world. There existed the largest Communist Party outside of Russia, and a literature and art based on the conditions of existence of the working-class. Internationalist, pacifist, revolutionary societies and organisations of all sorts flourished. Societies such as the League for the Rights of Man carried on energetic publicity campaigns against cases of injustice and abuse of power. Papers like the *Weltbühne*, under the editorship of the pacifist, Ossietski, laid bare social injustice, secrets of the High Command, etc. In art, literature, architecture the traditions and prejudices of the past were ruthlessly broken down, and new styles developed on the principle of the needs of modern society. The intellectuals of Europe flocked to see the buildings of the *Bauhaus*-School at Dessau, the productions of the Communist Piscator on the Berlin stage, the German film. The literature of the post-War period revolved round the problems of the working-class ; its social problems, as in Kayser and Toller, its individual problems, as in Döblin and Fallada. Culture seemed to be turning away from the middle-classes, and to be inaugurating the period of the working-class.

But this radical culture was very instable. What one heard and saw in Berlin was not what one heard and saw in the provinces ; in respectable middle-class families one met another culture, not very different from the plush interiors and Gothic porticos of the Wilhelmine era. In the country, long before Hitler's movement became powerful, one saw parades of Steel Helmets, the monarchist organisation. In the cinemas there was an infinite series of films apotheosising Frederick the Great, Queen Luise, and other national heroes. In whole districts of the provinces, especially in East Prussia, Pommerania, and Brandenberg, no newspapers but those of the Right were heard of. The Republic was as little able to create a harmonious culture as it was to reconcile the interests of the various social classes.

The Republic and the Possessing Classes

The subservience of the Republic to the powers of wealth is strikingly illustrated by the history of the Press since the War. The Hugenberg Press gives us an outstanding example. Hugenberg, as leader of the Party of the German Nationalists, had frankly reactionary aims—the crushing of the working-class parties and the restoration of the monarchy. Formerly General Director of Krupp's, he was usually able to establish a working agreement between Heavy Industry and the big landed interests. He took the lead in organising Company (" Yellow ") Trade Unions, with the specific aim of countering the plans of the Socialist Trade Unions. In the main, he was most successful in his Press policy. He first gained control of the Berlin daily, the *Lokalanzeiger*, with its quarter-million readership, then of the Press Agency, the *Telegraphenunion*, which sent out ready composed news to great numbers of provincial papers. It was estimated that in 1930 two-thirds of the German newspapers received their news more or less exclusively through Hugenberg's Agency, often reprinting it without comment. For many years he slowly bought up provincial papers, or made them dependent on his favours in advertisement. The type of paper was fairly recognisable. It was directed at the mass of people who were not organised industrially and were normally without very strong political interests, who were attracted by gossip and sensations. Hugenberg's politics were to foster this delight in scandal and to administer the Nationalist medicine in small, pleasantly tasting doses.

Hugenberg and his Party were not without imagination. Realising the growing importance of the cinema, they sought to turn it to their advantage. In 1927 the largest film company in Germany, the Ufa, was going begging. As a private enterprise it was unprofitable. The government refused to subsidise it. But the Ruhr industrialists were prepared to take it over as an instrument of their policy. Backed by a guarantee of millions from these industrialists Hugenberg acquired control of the Ufa. As far as business allowed—even Heavy Industry had to take the modern taste and German film tradition into account—propaganda for the Nationalist cause was made the aim of the German cinema. From this time dates what was recognised abroad as the artistic decline of the German film. But that long series of films on the German national heroes, on frivolous " light-hearted " subjects, was ample compensation for the Nationalist interests.

The control exerted by big financial interests over public opinion is seen most nakedly in the Press. Hugenberg's Press is not the only example. Time and time again the big newspapers changed hands, going to the highest bidder, the *Deutsche Allgemeine Zeitung* having a most chequered history. Sometimes all that was needed was financial support in times of difficulty. At various times bankers came to the support of a leading paper of the Catholic Centre, the *Kölnische Volkszeitung*; of democratic papers like the *Kölner Tageblatt*; of organs of the *Volkspartei* like the *Zeit.*

The *Reichstag* elections give another example of the part played by money in politics. The Social-Democrats alone published accounts of their electoral expenses. But a general view is given by the figures published by the *Berliner Montagspost* on May 21, 1928, as a result of an investigation into the costs of the elections of the Spring of that year. For the five greatest political parties in that election the following figures are significant [1]:

Party.	Election Costs. Marks.	Per vote. Marks.	Per seat in *Reichstag*. Marks.
Democrats	2,100,000	1.40	84,000
Volkspartei	3,750,000	1.40	83,000
German Nationals	5,000,000	1.15	68,000
Catholic Centre	1,250,000	·33	20,000
Social-Democrats	2,570,000	.27	16,500

To the expenses of the Social-Democrats one ought to add the cost of an army of permanent officials. These figures speak for themselves. Only extremely wealthy groups of interest could allow themselves the

[1] Quoted from R. Lewinsohn, *Das Geld in der Politik*, 1930.

propaganda and activity of the reactionary and "democratic" Parties. Any anti-capitalist Party had thus immense initial difficulties to overcome before it could even approach the masses. It is thus understandable that one of Hitler's chief tasks was to harangue and exhort Chambers of Commerce, Federations of Employers, etc. to enlist money on his side. In England, similarly, Sir Oswald Mosley's party is blessed with reserves of wealth, which show him to be in alliance with those dark forces of interest which shackle democratic thought and activity even in the accepted "democracies".

But the power of wealth in publicistic activities is chiefly important as being symptomatic of the whole social process in the period of the Republic. The National-Socialists called the 1918 Revolution a "Stock-Exchange Revolution", which gave power to international capital; the Dawes and Young Agreements are cited as evidence. But this view is false. The 1918 Revolution put power in the hands of *German* capital, and the financial and industrial policy of the Republic was directed by German capital to ensure the health of German capitalist economy. The main outlines of the history of the Republic show, in fact, how all the principles and provisions of the Constitution which tended towards socialism, all the promises of the Social-Democratic Party, were abandoned when the interests of capital demanded it.

In agriculture, the agreements with the former Ruling Houses, by which their property was largely ratified, was a first blow for the small peasants and land-workers. Something, however, seemed to be promised by the Land Settlement Law, passed on August 11, 1919. By this Law large estates over 100 hectares were to be restricted to a proportion of 10 per cent of the whole cultivated area of the various provinces. Where they formed more than 10 per cent, as in parts of Prussia, the part above 10 per cent was to be given to the State for division into small-holdings. The results were a complete fiasco. By 1922 not one-fifteenth of the amount of land due through this law had been delivered to the State. The rate of land-settlement did not materially increase in the following years—it would have taken something like a hundred years to accomplish even the modest programme of the Law of 1919! The big interests on the land, aided by their allies elsewhere, were able to defy the law. With regard to the *Fideikommisse*, lands held by big estate-owners in trust for the State, the Republic was even more accommodating. Many of these lands had been distributed just before and during the War, and the Weimar Constitution promised their dissolution (Art. 155). But a Prussian Order of only four months after November 1918 was already most conciliatory, stating that the *Fideikommisse* should be voluntarily dissolved by April 1, 1921, and that only after that date would the State step in. Then, in November 1920, another Order was made putting off the dissolution until after the death of the existing owner, in certain circumstances even of his heir. The control and organisation of the dissolution of these estates were left in the hands of the owning family, and the further ownership remained in the family. Similar arrangements were made in other States than Prussia. Poor peasants and agricultural labourers were cheated of their hopes of sharing in the *Fideikommisse*.

We should contrast this with the situation of the land-workers. Social-Democracy had promised an eight-hour day for workers. A provisional agreement of January 24, 1919, fixed the maximum hours for land-workers at eight hours per day for four months, ten hours for four months, and eleven hours for the remaining third of the year. But even this maximum was not observed, and after a few sporadic strikes matters settled down as if there had been no State-regulation of hours. At most the land-workers gained an increase of pay over the pre-War rates, though a fair proportion of their wages was still paid in kind.

In industry and finance, too, the Republic gave full sway to the big interests, imposing only the most modest of checks in favour of the working-classes. On the whole, in spite of the invective of the National-Socialists against the bankers, it was Big Industry which ruled. Since the end of the nineteenth century, the princes of industry had overhauled the lords of finance. The inflation finally hurled the financiers into the class of the small fry. Some speculators, like Hugo Herzfeld, tried to make a fortune by buying up material goods, factories, etc. at good prices, but they mostly showed themselves incapable of profiting by their purchases in the deflation-period following 1923. Those who gained by the inflation were, apart from mortgage-holders who paid off their debts in depreciated money, the owners of industry, especially those who took advantage of the inflation to consolidate their property. A peculiar effect of the inflation was the formation of "vertical" trusts, concerns which combined factories of all types, from those mining raw material to those producing the finished goods, including systems of transport and industries working by-products. Stinnes is the characteristic figure. His concern included coal-mines, steel-works, shipping-lines, electrical-works, oil-wells, paper-works, newspapers (the *Deutsche Allgemeine Zeitung* belonged to him for a while), and finally banks. Although his concern was unwieldy, it held together while he lived, and his power was enormous. When, in 1924, he gave the signal, the Ruhr coal industry posted up notices to the effect that they were abandoning the eight-hour day, and the State was unable to do anything but accept their decision. It was largely under his leadership that the delivery of goods under the Reparations section of the Treaty of Versailles was made a matter for private agreement between German industrialists and Foreign Powers.

Stinnes, the admired of the National-Socialists, represents Big Industry in its nakedness, hectoring the Democratic State. Usually the princes of industry were more patient, less challenging, accumulating their power around them in their trusts and putting up men of straw as their political mouthpiece. Even before the War German industry was noted for its high degree of trustification. The inflation was turned to advantage by further development in this way. Hugo Herzfeld, for instance, contributed largely to the trustification of the potash industry, Jacob Michael of the chemical industry. Then, after the

Dawes Plan was signed, German industry began to equip itself to pay the Reparations agreed upon. An enormous export-surplus was necessary, and the democratic government relied on capitalist industry to realise it. Rationalisation took place rapidly and ruthlessly, and the ultimate principle of rationalisation is trustification. Foreign capital poured into Germany with the first signs of its prosperity, and hastened the process, the political form of which was Stresemann with his policy of " Fulfillment ". Democratic Germany produced that system of vast combines, the Steel, Coal, Chemical, Potash, Electrical, Trusts, etc., interconnected by mutual holdings, to whom the banks were subservient, and whose interests directed those of the State's.

Not merely did the Republic tolerate this process of trustification ; it was based on the trusts. Two of the biggest industrial groups, the Potash and the Coal industries were organised under a *Reich* directory, so that the decisions of the industry were binding on the government. The presence of governmental representatives on these bodies could not essentially modify their policy, as this was dictated by economic, capitalistic realities ; they merely lent the decisions of the industry State authority. The same situation exists in England in the Public Corporations, particularly in such a body as the London Transport Board. Governments are as ineffectual to control such bodies as Roosevelt in U.S.A. has been with regard to the Ford, Mills, and other trusts. The position of the workers in such industries is evident from the bitter strikes which have broken out, strikes which are either directly or indirectly aimed at the policy of the governments. Such strikes were those in the German coal area in 1919, 1920, and 1921, or the great nation-wide strikes of 1928—to be compared with the strikes in U.S.A. in 1934 against the Roosevelt industrial policy, or the strikes of the London Transport workers.

Thus the German democracy built up within itself gigantic industrial powers on whose benevolence the State depended. Social-Democracy actively aided in this process. While favouring the form of Public Corporations, they supported trustification, since the greater profitability of trustified industry meant higher wages for the workers. Even in Social-Democratic circles Ford was considered an object-lesson of organisation, with his high profits and high wages. Their attitude is well illustrated by the sale of the Match Monopoly to the Swedish monopolist Kreuger in 1929. This was advocated and carried through by Hilferding, the Social-Democratic finance-minister, as a "good piece of business".[1] Having accepted the principle of capitalism, the Social-Democrats carried it to its logical conclusion. Theoretically they tried to prove that trustification was a step towards socialisation, but ignored the fact that they were organising and concentrating capitalist power, which when necessary would sweep them and all working-class representation away. Their politics forced them to deny the possibility of an economic

[1] Kreuger was held up as a model by a young English Socialist, A. L. Rouse, in his book, *Politics and the Younger Generation*, pp. 46–7.

crisis which would show up to their followers the hollowness of their pretensions and withdraw from them the toleration of a desperate industry.

The Foreign Policy of the Republic had the same origins as its industrial policy. The National-Socialists have always represented the policy of "Fulfillment"; the acceptance of the Treaty of Versailles, with its corollaries the Dawes and Young Plans, as treachery of the "internationalist" parties practised on German economy. But the influx of capital which this policy brought redounded for the time to the benefit of industry. The goverment had to consider vitally the health of capitalism, and loans poured in from abroad. Although, in some instances, foreign capital won control of parts of German industry—for instance, some concerns in the electrical industry came under American control—on the whole this was not so. German capital became enriched and much more ambitious through the foreign loans, and won a stronger position in the *Reich.* True, taxation was heavier and greater burdens lay on the lower middle-class and the working-class; but the relative position of German industry within the State was infinitely stronger. Events have shown, since the suspension of payments on German foreign debts, that foreign capital in Germany, far from being able to dictate Germany's policy, is dependent on the prosperity of German industry.

The Republic and the Working-class

What, however, of the Republic's policy towards the working-class? There seemed to be many safeguards in the Constitution for the workers, its social legislation was held up as a model to all other countries. The Trade Unions, the organisations of the workers, had the legal right of representing their members on local and national bodies. Special Conciliation bodies existed, on which the workers were represented, to settle questions arising between master and man. In all factories over a certain size a Workers' Factory Council was elected, to deal directly with the management. Outwardly, too, in the period before the crisis of 1929, the situation of the mass of the people in Germany seemed prosperous. Largely owing to the loans from abroad an extensive campaign of building was entered upon. Everywhere one saw spacious new municipal buildings, Welfare and Savings Bank offices, new blocks of workers' flats. In many towns and communes the Social-Democrats were the largest party, and set their pride in increasing the public wealth in the form of public buildings. German Social-Democracy was looked on as a paragon among all the members of the Second International.

But there was a reverse to this happy picture. The workers themselves were often not satisfied with the bargains struck by their Social-Democratic or Trade Union leaders. The first collective agreements on wages between Trade Unions and coal owners were greeted by a series of strikes, and the strikes were therefore directed against the Unions. There was general dismay at the lack of a concrete socialistic policy, at the lack of power of the Trade Unions, which resulted in a great falling-off of membership. In 1920 the Free Trade Unions had a membership of 8 millions, which by 1931 had fallen to four and a half; and many of those who stayed in the Unions did so entirely because of the insurance benefits accruing, and not out of any faith in the politics of the Unions. By 1932 the leadership of the Unions expressly disavowed any pretensions to a working-class policy as such, claiming only to serve the "social" needs of their members. In 1929 a Social-Democratic leader declared that the aim of Social-Democracy was to "make itself at home in capitalism"; but this passive negative attitude implied great activity against those elements in the working-class which aimed at socialism.

The history of the Factory Councils illustrates extremely well the limitations of working-class power within capitalistic society. In the Weimar Constitution it had been ordained that Factory Councils should be set up, though the relations of these Councils to the Trade Unions had not been defined. The Councils showed themselves, in practice, to be on the whole much more militant than the Unions. They knew the exact situation on the job, they were directly under the eyes of the workers, and results had to be reported at once. They had little or no administrative responsibility, and consequently considered their only interest to be the welfare of the workers in the factory. Communist influence on the Councils was strong, and attempts were made to call annually national Conferences of Factory Councils, in order there to hammer out a national working-class policy, in opposition to that of Social-Democracy and the Trade Unions.

The Trade Unions laboured from the first to get the Factory Councils under their control. They feared the Councils as an alternative leadership, and as a leadership based on the recognition of the class-war. The Councils were easily disposed to call strikes, with varying success, an expression of opposition to the regime which the Trade Unions could condone only in some instances. The Unions endeavoured as a general policy to establish in all factories their own list of candidates for the Councils, and were largely successful in this, for they could offer in support of their candidates legal experience and financial reserves. They boycotted strikes called without their authority, and as the Councils themselves had no reserves of money from which to share out strike-pay, these " wild " strikes were often a failure, resulting very often in the dismissal of the more militant workers. Again, disputes between men and employers had usually to go before a Conciliation Board or Court of summary jurisdiction, and here the legal machinery of the Unions made itself indispensable to the workers.

Apart from the period immediately following the establishment of Factory Councils, and the restless period of the inflation, 1923 and 1924, the Unions on the whole controlled the policy of the Councils. The importance of this was very considerable. The Unions, as responsible national organisations, were far more willing to make allowance for the general prosperity of the State, i.e. of capitalism, than were isolated Factory Councils. They were ready to collaborate with industry in its rationalising policy.[1] This meant, however, that workers who lost their jobs or whose conditions worsened under rationalisation were prevented from opposing the employers, and lost their trust in the Unions, perhaps in the whole working-class cause. The Factory Councils were in effect no satisfactory defence of the men. An objective, detailed study of the Councils yielded the following conclusion : " The degree to which the powers (of the Factory Councils) can be enforced in practice and the use made of the facilities provided (by statute) are chiefly dependent upon those general economic forces which decide, when it comes to a trial of strength, whether the employing class as a whole or the employees as a whole have got the upper hand in industrial relations." [2] Built within the framework of capitalism, the Factory Councils could only protect the employees as far as the laws of capitalist economy allowed.

In the German Republic the employers had the whip-hand. By every means in their power they tried to get rid of this irksome institution, the Factory Council. Militant members of the Councils were rendered harmless by dismissal. Others were bribed or bullied. The Balance Sheet, which had to be presented to the Factory Councils for scrutiny, was drawn up in such a way that only patient examination

[1] Cf. the opening paragraph of the Resolution of the 12th Free Trade Union Congress, 1925 : " The solution of the economic problems with which the country is faced can only be attained by means of the democratisation of the economic system, *coupled with* the rationalisation of labour and improvements in the technique and organisation of business."

[2] C. W. Guillebaud, *The Works Council*, 1928, p. 227.

by experts could elucidate the real situation of the firm. Above all a resolute front was made against that clause of the Constitution which promised District Workers' Councils and a National Workers' Council. Despite repeated protests and appeals from working-class bodies these never came into existence. The State flouted its own promises. For the working-class the Constitution was transformed from a definition of rights into a programme of cajolery.

Much indignant expletive has been spent on the financial " scandals " of the Republic. The Barmat, Kutisker, Sklarek swindles have been cited, especially by National-Socialists, as evidence of the rottenness of German democracy—and in these scandals State institutions such as the Prussian State Bank, *Reichstag* and municipal deputies have been implicated. But it is false to draw a distinction between " honest " capitalism and " dishonest " on the basis of these scandals. Especially in the period after the inflation high interest rates and high dividends were common in German business. Levels are fixed by the conditions of business, and all participants are anxious to profit. The principles which make honest and dishonest capitalism are essentially the same. The " scandal " of the Republic was the disparity in power between the classes owning capital and those owning none. The " scandal " was, that Social-Democracy upheld this democracy as a means to socialism, contenting themselves with proposing further steps towards " industrial democracy "—steps which, like their proposal to turn the National Economic Council into an industrial parliament, would simply have hastened the process of concentration of power in the hands of Big Industry.[1] And to crown all, this system of the Republic led to the Crisis of 1929, which brought not merely economic misery to millions of Germans, but also the withdrawal of most of the political liberties guaranteed by the Constitution ; the system led to its own abdication, to the dictatorship of Hitler.

[1] A similar plan for an " industrial parliament " was popular in National-Socialist circles.

CHAPTER III

THE CRISIS

In Germany, despite the hollowness of the pretensions of democracy, violent mass-opposition to the Republic ebbed away after 1924 until the world crisis which began in 1929. The stabilisation of the mark, the regulation of Reparations in the Dawes Plan, led to an immense influx of foreign capital into Germany in the form of loans and private investment—the foreign indebtedness of Germany in 1932 was still 19 milliards of marks. German industry expanded and built up a big foreign market. Though unemployment remained relatively high—task-work was never abandoned in the whole post-War period, and occupied on an average at least 50,000 unemployed—wages rose considerably between 1924 and 1929, largely as the result of extensive strikes in 1928. In this year 691 strikes were engaged on as compared with about half that number in the years preceding and following 1928, the workers winning 187 completely, and gaining partial concessions in 304. In this period of abundance of capital, local and central authorities entered on that spectacular campaign of building which brought admiring visitors from all over the world. Hospitals, scientific institutes, railway-stations, public buildings of all sorts were built to meet modern requirements; and this increase in public wealth was one of the most positive achievements of the Republic. Under these conditions the Social-Democratic Party recovered some of its lost votes, so that in 1928 Hermann Müller, the Social-Democratic leader, became German Chancellor.

Prosperity gave the majority of the Germans a faith in democracy ; Henry Ford of Detroit was their witch-doctor. But moral stability depended on economic. In 1929 the cloudburst occurred which was to reshape the contours of the country. In September 1930 there could be no doubt of the earnestness of the threat to democratic thought and the democratic system. Hitler polled 6 million votes, the Communists 3,850,000. The Social-Democratic Party lost 2 millions. The Democratic Parties began their rapid career of dissolution, the climax to which was to be the assumption of power by Hitler in 1933. It is clear that the world-crisis, as it affected Germany, cannot be looked on as a merely economic phenomenon. But it is sometimes overlooked that the crisis has bitten deep in its effects on the whole political structure of the world. Trustification and cartellisation has proceeded apace ; in U.S.A. the Anti-Trust laws have been suspended. The most stringent measures have been everywhere taken, in the form of State subsidies and tariffs, to isolate national economic life from international competition ; and a corresponding change in outlook has been consciously and unconsciously engendered. Nationalism has replaced liberal internationalism as the philosophy of the dominant classes ; in England and France " National " governments were formed. The internationalism of the Socialist Parties has paled more than ever to a verbalism. Recovery from the crisis, partial as it is, does not mean a restoration of the old order in any country, but the sacrifice of many old principles and liberties, a sharpened struggle between nations and classes. The course of German politics during the crisis shows us this general process in its nakedness.

I do not intend here to attempt to analyse the causes of the crisis. It is, of course, not restricted to any particular nation, but is a crisis in the whole capitalist economy of the world. It was brought on by competition in capitalist industry, competition between industries, between nations. The method adopted everywhere to overcome the crisis has been a strengthening of the resistant power of industry on a national basis. On the one hand industries have been cartellised, trustified, often under State-leadership; marketing areas have been closed to foreign competition, and production restricted; on the other hand, partly through this process of cartellisation, partly through the application of rigorous laws, the resistance of the workers to wage-cuts, part-time, etc. has been weakened. It was inevitable that Germany, dependent more than most countries on foreign markets, and already highly organised industrially, should suffer more than other countries through the crisis, and should have to adopt more desperate methods to remedy the situation.

The structure of German industry had been deeply affected by the need for making Reparation payments. Even before the War Germany could pride itself on the high degree of organisation of its industry. In some branches cartels were perfect enough to allow for a national policy in the foreign market and to control prices at home. The inflation period had strengthened this tendency towards monopoly. Under the Young Plan all emphasis had to be laid on maintaining an excess of exports over imports. The need for cheap mass-production led to rationalisation of production and distribution, and to trustification. The general result was that by 1930 there were 1,455 nation-wide combines and cartels in Germany, apart from the many provincial and district associations. This cartellisation was not able to hold up the progress of the crisis. Industrial production in 1932 was 60 per cent of that in 1928. The number of hours worked, which reached in 1929 75 per cent of capacity, fell in 1932 to under 40 per cent. Production in the most important and most highly organised industry, iron and steel, dropped in 1932 to about a quarter of that in 1929. At the same time the crisis hastened the process of trustification. The number of bankruptcies grew from 10,595 in 1928, 13,180 in 1929, 15,486 in 1930, to 19,254 in 1931. But the big concerns were not seriously affected. The movement in Joint-Stock companies between 1930 and 1931 is strikingly illustrated by the following table [1] :

	Joint-Stock Co.'s with Capital of:						
	5–50 thousand m.	50–100 thousand m.	100–500 thousand m.	500 thousand to 1 mill. m.	1–5 mill. m.	5–20 mill. m.	Over 20 mill. m.
No. in 1930	91	63	258	102	221	70	56
No. in 1931	67	57	231	91	167	124	56

[1] From *Statistisches Jahrbuch für das deutsche Reich*, 1932.

It is clear from this table that, while smaller companies fell victims to the crisis, the number of larger concerns actually increased, the amount of nominal capital invested in concerns of from 5 to 20 millions of marks increasing from 663 millions in 1930 to 842 millions in 1931.

Under the chancellorship of Brüning, vigorous efforts were made to isolate Germany from the effects of the world fall in production and in prices. By imposing enormous tariffs he made Germany into a market for its own produce—he boasted that as far as agriculture was concerned Germany was insulated from the world. All sorts of differentiation against foreign imports were introduced in the hope of keeping German factories busy. However, the sensational bankruptcy of the *Darmstaedter und National Bank* (the *Danat*) and of the great woollen trust, *Nordwolle*, in the Summer of 1931 revealed the insecurity of the German position. The State was forced to step in as guarantor and merge the *Dresdner Bank* with the *Danat*, to save a worse crash ; and by taking over the debts of the *Danat* it acquired control of smaller banks and industrial enterprises.[1] In 1932, when the owner of the majority of the shares of the largest German steel trust, the *Allgemeiner Stahl Verein*, was preparing to sell out to French interests, Brüning's national policy forced him to buy them for the nation. As often, the State showed itself a bad

[1] By 1932 the State owned 90 per cent of the capital stock of the *Dresdner und Danat Bank*, 70 per cent of the *Commerz und Privat Bank*, and 35 per cent of the *Deutsche Bank*, i.e. the State had nominal control ot the biggest German banks.

bargainer, and a whole host of big industrialists, tired of their barren capital, longingly offered their shares to the State. But though Brüning did acquire certain mining shares, he showed himself not in the least eager to effect in this way a nationalisation of industry. The position of power he thus acquired in industry was never used to carry through a national as opposed to an individualistic policy.[1] Brüning's most positive economic acts were in different spheres. He was successful in his representations to the Allied Powers that Reparations, as settled in the Young Plan of 1930, were a fatal burden on Germany. In August 1931 the first Moratorium was arranged, being the first step to the final settlement of August 1932. And early in 1932 he was able to effect a compulsory reduction of the rates of interest on agricultural loans, which constituted a temporary relief to land owners.

The effects of the crisis were felt in all their bitterness by the wage-earning classes. At the end of 1928 76·2 per cent of the industrial workers were employed; at the end of 1929, 71·9 per cent; at the end of 1930, 67·5 per cent; at the end of 1931, 61 per cent. Unemployment at the end of 1931 was reckoned at 4,500,000 with benefit 680,000 without any form of support. In January 1933 the number of registered unemployed reached 6 millions, the number of unregistered being generally estimated at a further 2 millions. The Means Test was applied sternly. The wage-rates of those workers still employed fell rapidly, dropping by 1932 to between

[1] Hitler also refuses to allow the State to control industrial enterprises as a private shareholder would.

one-half and one-third of the 1928 level. Short time was general. The Trade Union leaders, acquiescing in Brüning's policy, could offer no opposition to the measures taken by industry to maintain itself. Strikes became more and more rare. The age limit for the Old Age pension was dropped, so that many workers of 60 withdrew from the labour market to live on this pittance.

At the same time, the policy of the successive crisis-governments, of Müller, then of Brüning, had the result of making the standard of living go up. The control of prices by industry and agriculture was reinforced by State authority. Under the Social-Democratic chancellor prices were fixed for sugar, wheat, rye, and pigs. Big subsidies were paid to producers of sugar and rye. In February 1930 the price of rye on the open market was 91 marks per ton; in the home market it was 163 marks. The home price of sugar was three times that of the open price. The milling industry was sheltered by the enforcement of home-milling for home-grown wheat. The distribution of home-grown maize was undertaken by the State. As a result of these governmental measures retail prices remained high while wages and unemployment benefit rates dropped. The retail price of wheat was higher in 1931 than in 1928, '29, or '30; that of sugar rose to 71 pfennig per kilo in 1931 as compared with roughly 60 pfennig in the years preceding. The whole cost of living figures did not drop appreciably till late in 1932; rents were at their highest level in 1931, as also the calculated cost of heating, lighting, and travelling fares. The consumption of milk fell 8 per cent from 1930 to 1931, and a further 10 per cent in the following year, a horrifying sign of the impoverishment of the masses.

A special feature of this gigantic industrial depression was the unemployment of the professional classes, which are as a rule immune from economic anxiety. The decrease of production threw thousands of skilled engineers out of work. In the interests of economy doctors were dismissed and freshly graduated medical men were not given jobs. The restriction of the labour market induced many boys to study at the universities, in the hope that things would be better later on. The only result was that the universities became overcrowded, and unemployment among the "studied" classes increased. It was officially reckoned, on the basis of the figures for 1929, that there would be 13,778 surplus trained teachers in 1934. After this date the policy of economy was pursued to such an extent, for instance by increasing the size of classes, that the surplus was actually two or three times this figure in 1933. It is not surprising that the number of suicides in Germany rose from the appalling figure of 16,665 in 1929 to that of 18,934 in 1932.

The elections of 1930 reflected the desperation into which the masses of the German people were falling. The combined democratic vote held only a slight majority in the *Reichstag*. Extraordinary measures had to be taken. And so, soon after Brüning of the Centre Catholic Party had been made chancellor, use was made of Paragraph 48 of the Constitution. Laws were no longer debated and passed by the

Reichstag, but decreed by Presidential authority. For the next two years and more, until the " National Revolution ", democratic Germany was to be ruled by virtue of this paragraph. The *Reichstag* met only at long intervals, in order to pass by the usual narrow majority a vote of confidence in the government. The President, Hindenburg, by whose will use was made of these emergency powers, ceased to be a figurehead, and held the destiny of Germany in his hands. Democracy was forced, in order to save itself, to renounce democratic methods. But the discrediting of the idea of popular representation did not discredit those Parties which made the *Reichstag* ineffective—the Communists and the National-Socialists. They continued to grow ; and " democracy ", the sort of democracy realised in the democratic Republic, and struggling in death-throes under the Brüning dictatorship, began to stink in German nostrils.

CHAPTER IV

THE ORGANISATION OF THE NATIONAL-SOCIALIST PARTY

HITLERISM proper arose immediately after the War in a nucleus of old soldiers, desperate opponents of the new Republic. In his youth Hitler was a boy of pretensions who had been forced to undertake many sorts of jobs in order to earn a living. Wherever he had met the doctrines of the class-struggle or the class-organisations of the proletariat, the Trade Unions, he had been repelled in his innermost heart. He had learnt to feel an equal repugnance for Jewish bankers and newspaper owners, by whom in his view the world is controlled, and severely censured the Crowned Heads of Europe for tolerating this alien dominance. He was, even before the War, intent on reform, on strengthening the arm of national control and breaking the power of Jews and Marxists. An Austrian born, he believed from the first in the necessity of joining all German-speaking peoples in one powerful nation.

With the Revolution of 1918 his worst fears were realised. The Socialists had come to power. Out of his first prostration the vigorous nationalism of the newly formed *Reichswehr* rescued him. In conjunction with Gottfried Feder, now Commissioner for Land Settlement, who demonstrated to him the power and workings of international finance capital, he conceived the idea of rejuvenating the authoritarian State, and shortly afterwards had his first taste of power after the overthrow of the Workers' Republic of Bavaria. His first positive political experience was gained on the Commission of Inquiry into the subversive forces in his regiment.

Shortly afterwards Hitler joined up, as the seventh member, with an extreme Nationalist Party in Munich. Into this Party he introduced new methods and new aims. Instead of fearing the masses, he saw the need for challenging the masses and making the party into a mass-party. Hence the new name, decided after much discussion—the National-Socialist German Workers' Party ; he himself explains in his book *My Struggle* how he realised it was necessary to attract the masses by such popular words as " socialist " and " workers ", in spite of his repugnance for everything that socialism stands for. The political Party he turned into an Association for Struggle (*Kampfgemeinschaft*) ; and instead of democratic methods and control, the authoritarian principle is followed. The leader is entrusted with full responsibility, and the whole gamut of sub-leaders are responsible to their superiors, not their followers—an organisation on militaristic lines.[1] Hence arose a movement of great energy and force, based on action and a scorn of debating, with complete obedience to the commands of its leaders.

[1] See Hitler, *Mein Kampf*, ed. in one volume, 1933, pp. 377 ff. It is not advisable to refer to the English translation, as important passages are omitted.

Militarists and Monarchists

Hitler's own account of the rise of his Party, in particular of the development of the Storm Troops, is, to say the least, misleading. After the War there were in Germany many illegal military bands, under the leadership of monarchist officers, which carried on a secret terror against democracy. These Freikorps aimed at overthrowing the government by military means, and individual terror was their tactic. To them Liebknecht and Luxemburg, Rathenau and Erzberger, and hundreds of lesser known champions of the democratic State or of the working-classes owed their death. Their leaders were in close touch with the *Reichswehr*, and were provided by the *Reichswehr* with money and arms. But these *Freikorps* were secret societies, and their tactics showed that they were largely divorced from the masses. At that time a military dictatorship such as they planned could be met and defeated by the forces of the working-class, as the *Kapp Putsch* showed. Hitler saw the need of creating, through a political mass-movement, the atmosphere in which the aims of the *Freikorps* could be nurtured.

While, then, he introduced a demagogic tone into the political Party he had joined, he gave it also an organisation approximating to that of the *Freikorps*—the Storm Troops. The invention of the Storm Troops was not such a stroke of pure genius as he represents it in *Mein Kampf*; it has a very material basis. Members of the *Freikorps*, in particular of the

Ehrhardt Brigade, which had been proscribed for political murders, were anxious for a job. In Hitler they found an allied soul. They were taken into his Party ; but these fiery militarists needed something better than political propaganda. They were organised as special military troops, under the leadership of the political Party, i.e. of Hitler. Hitler defines the Storm Troops first as organised room-stewards whose task it was to prevent opponents from breaking up Hitler's meetings. But there is no doubt that they were aggressive, not defensive, from the first. In the course of 1920 various meetings of Hitler's opponents were smashed up by these " room-stewards ". The fusion of rowdies with the officers of the *Freikorps* produced the Storm Troops, which were formally founded at the end of 1921. Their first leader was a former lieutenant in the *Ehrhardt Brigade*, and at his side stood notable terrorists, Captain Killinger and Captain Hoffmann. Not averse from exercising violence at meetings, these men had higher ambitions. From the moment of their dominance in the Storm Troops a more ruthless course towards insurrection was steered by the Hitler Party, to end with the *Putsch* of 1923.

In his book, Hitler attributes the growth of his Party from 1920 to the power of eloquence and truth, and to its excellent organisation. How was it, however, that his fulminations against the established order, his use and advocacy of force, were tolerated by the government ? Here he has drawn a veil. But others have not respected his silence. Especially from the legal proceedings following on his 1923 *Putsch* do we gain an insight into the true forces behind his rise.

These were the Bavarian government and the army.[1]

Since the Bavarian Commune had been crushed in 1919 by the army, a strongly reactionary government had been in power. Kahr, the premier, a monarchist in sympathies, had marked his appreciation of the action of the army by keeping up good relations with all organisations of the Right. His Police-President, Pöhner, was a member of Hitler's Party, as was also Frick, a high official in the Civil Service. Kahr systematically protected the National-Socialist Party and its members from all impeachments from democratic quarters. Repeatedly he entered into negotiations with Hitler, his aim being to enlist Hitler's support in a war of liberation of Bavaria against Berlin. Hitler entered upon the 1923 *Putsch* in the belief that Kahr would open all gates to him ; and only when Kahr saw that might was on the side of Berlin did he take sides against the *Putsch*.

The relations between the Bavarian government and the National-Socialist Party were determined by a much stronger force, the army. Kahr had been put in the saddle by the army, and was dependent in his decisions on the lead given by army officers, in particular by Von Lossow, the Officer Commanding the Bavarian divisions. On the other hand, the army undertook the financing of the Irregulars. Captain Röhm, who had considerable influence with Lossow,

[1] See *Der Hitler Prozess*, 1924 ; and the Report of the Committee of Investigation of the Bavarian *Landtag*, entitled, *Hitler und Kahr*, published by the Social-Democratic Party, Munich, 1928.

was a member of the National-Socialist Party, and in effective command of the Storm Troops. Hitler himself did not leave the army until some time after he had established himself as a leading speaker of the Party. Some of the ex-officers in the Storm Troops were salaried (illegally of course) by Röhm out of army funds. General Von Epp rendered a great service to the Party when he put in its hands sufficient funds to buy the *Völkischer Beobachter*, the newspaper which has remained since then the chief organ of the Party.

Apart from these valuable financial services, the *Reichswehr* gained military control over the Storm Troops. Along with other illegal military bands, they were allowed to carry out military exercises with the *Reichswehr.* They received instruction in modern strategy and the use of modern weapons, and were provided with arms. So close were the relations between Storm Troops and army that on one occasion, Storm Troopers " raided " certain barracks in Bavaria and carried off army stores (May 1, 1923). When the government prohibited a planned demonstration of the Party on January 27, 1923, the army used its influence to get the prohibition raised. As a result the Party became more and more the instrument of army politics. Röhm's aim was a military *coup d'état.* It was he who established Hitler as the Leader, who crushed all rival factions in the National-Socialist Party. And it was he who created a United Front of all the illegal military organisations.

Under these auspices the rising of November 9, 1923, was attempted. The militarists planned and controlled it. Ludendorff, the old general whose prestige was then higher than Hindenburg's, was the political figurehead. The Storm Troops showed their true face as soldiers of the Counter Revolution. The strategy was false, however. The High Command of the *Reichswehr* was ready to crush the rising. The Bavarian Command and government saw that the moment was unpropitious, and backed out at the last minute. The Bavarian police fired on the insurgents instead of embracing them, the ranks broke and the rebels ran. Fourteen were killed. Hitler was captured a day or two later, Göring was released on parole and fled over the frontier.

The ensuing trial was a farce, for the rebels who had attempted to throw out the constituted government were accorded gracious treatment. Ludendorff was treated with deference. Hitler received one year's imprisonment in a fortress—the lightest type of imprisonment. Storm Troopers who had invaded and damaged a newspaper office were let off scot-free because of their " honourable motives "—like the British Fascists who were let off by an English judge because they were " good fellows ". But the effects of the *Putsch* were far-reaching. The connexions between *Reichswehr* generals and National-Socialist Party were for the time being broken off—to be re-established only in 1932. The Party became more a political, less a military, organisation. Röhm went into obscurity, later becoming military advisor to the Bolivian government. For several years the Party struggled in rough waters, before its new course became clear.

New Masters—Industry

The new line differed organisationally from the old in the subordination of the Storm Troops. The purely militaristic tactic of a *Putsch* was now impossible, since Hitler received no encouragement from the army. Under successive leaders the Storm Troops threatened to dominate the Party, and successive crises led to the dismissal of S.A. leaders like Von Pfeffer and Stennes. In 1925 Hitler guaranteed his own position against the pretensions of the S.A. by forming a special guard, the *Schutzstaffeln* (S.S.), whose aim was to protect the Leader. The S.S. were forbidden to take part in political discussion. Their principles were defined by Himmler, their chief, as loyalty, obedience, and comradeliness. Even their private lives were devoted to the Cause, and later special orders were published controlling them in such matters as marriage, smoking, etc. They are the Leader's private army, the foil to the Party's army, the S.A. Their uniforms are black, with a skull and cross-bones as badge. Their true function became evident in 1934, when they were used to quell the S.A. revolt of Röhm.

Politically the National-Socialist Party has never had the unity popularly ascribed to it. From 1925 two main trends can be distinguished, one led by Gregor Strasser and one by Hitler, and there were frequent clashes. Strasser, a Bavarian chemist, held a subordinate position in the Party in Bavaria, and had played a modest part in the *Putsch*. After 1925 he undertook a series of agitational journeys in North

Germany, where he established a number of loosely connected Party groups. To some extent swayed by the prevailing radicalism in the industrial centres of the North and West, Strasser emphasised the socialistic aspect of National-Socialism. He declared war on the privileges of the rich and repudiated those alliances on which Hitlerism had hitherto thrived, alliances with officers and monarchists. He discovered Goebbels in Westphalia, and Goebbels added his voice to the radicals. The banks, the trusts, were linked up with the Marxists as the object of National-Socialist hatred, whereas with Hitler the chief enemies had been the working-class and democratic government. Goebbels in these years went so far as to tone down the Party's Anti-Semitism, and to distinguish between the " criminal " wealthy Jews, and the " virtuous " poor Jews. These radical theories, and the loose organisation in the North, threatened Hitler's prestige seriously, and at times a split in the Party between North and South, Strasser and Hitler, seemed inevitable.[1]

Hitler's line, since his imprisonment, was one of very practical politics. At the end of 1924 his Party had only 12 members in the *Reichstag*. His old patrons, the *Reichswehr*, had turned away from him. Little money came in from subscriptions, and it was vitally necessary for him to gather money. And so he made his chief propaganda in moneyed circles. He had already talked before industrialists. In the Hitler

[1] For further detail see Konrad Heiden, *Geschichte des Nationalsozialismus*, a book which has invaluable detailed information concerning the history of the National-Socialist movement.

trial of 1924 a Munich industrialist, Aust, declared: "In order to discuss Hitler's economic plans a discussion took place in the office of Privy Councillor Kuhlo, a syndic of the Bavarian Federation of Industry. The latter, Dr. Noll, further the chairman of the Federation of Industry, and myself were present. As a consequence of this discussion another was arranged in the Herren Club (an exclusive club to which the best German society belongs) . . . and later a bigger meeting in the Business-men's Casino. Herr Hitler made a speech on his aims, with much applause. Some gentlemen, who were not acquainted with Hitler, expressed their satisfaction by handing me donations to pass on to Hitler." During a short journey to Berlin in 1922 Hitler spoke in the National Club, and met there Borsig, the owner of the Locomotive works, who later provided him liberally with money.

From the Summer of 1926 Hitler pursued these methods more fully. If he was to control the restless elements in his Party, he could do so only by holding the purse-strings. In June he spoke before a group of industrial leaders in Essen, in December in Essen and Königswinter. In the following April 400 industrialists came to hear him speak in Essen. A newspaper belonging to these circles expressed pleasure that Hitler asked of the industrialists nothing that was not practicable. In the question of the financing of Hitler's movement statements of his former allies or of former members of his movement throw light on matters otherwise kept in closest mystery. His former ally Von Ramin, in the *Deutsches Tageblatt* of

March 1, 1927, writes of Hitler's patrons thus: "I have even sat at one table with Herr Hitler and such patrons. . . . When he was only the 'drummer-boy' and not a caricature of Mussolini, he did not merely take money from a well-known Berlin politician (Borsig is meant), but also fetched his instructions from the latter's office." Or again, in 1929 Captain H. von Mücke resigned from the National-Socialist Party because of the influence of the big textile-manufacturer Mutschmann. In an open letter of August 3, 1929, he declared that Mutschmann dominated the Party in Saxony—"it being an open secret, that the influence of Herr Mutschmann is due to the fact that, being a rich manufacturer, he has laid Herr Hitler under a financial obligation to him". Hitler's "patrons" themselves cannot forbear an occasional cheer. In the *Tag* of August 22, 1929, we read in an article by Kirdorf, the leader of the Westphalian Coal-Trust, a reference to the "comforting" development of the Storm Troopers. In a statement published in several newspapers Krupp von Bohlen complained that, in the Presidential Elections of 1932, a number of industrialists belonging to the *Gruppe Nordwest* had financed Hitler. These sums ran into millions. As the Party grew, funds became more and more necessary. Hitler declared in April 1932 to the *Evening Standard* correspondent that 300,000 S.A. men were unemployed. According to the paper, *Zeitnotizen*, each active unemployed Storm Trooper received 3 marks per day. This means an enormous current expenditure, even if we modify the figures somewhat. In this last period of Hitlerism, lack of money meant the crumbling of the movement. It was the captain of the Steel-Trust, Fritz Thyssen, who from 1930 secured for Hitler the necessary sums. Landowners also paid their mite to Hitler's funds. The German Nationalists complained in 1932 that the Brown House in Breslau was fitted out by the money of big landowners (*Berliner Tageblatt*, January 20).

A movement does not receive money without making obligations. While Hitlerite propaganda was irresponsible, the main line of the Party was kept parallel to that of big industry. Here Hitler came into conflict with Strasser as the representative of the more radical policy. The first conflict took place on the question of the expropriation of the former Ruling Houses. At the Party Congress in Bamberg (1926) the Party, under Hitler's leadership, decided not to vote for the expropriation of the princes, and Strasser was given a rebuff. Hitler was skilful enough to win over into his own camp Goebbels, who saw where the power and the money lay, and later in the year Goebbels was made District Leader of Berlin, directly responsible to Hitler. Thus important steps were made to check the radicalism of the North and the danger of a split between Berlin and Munich. Strasser did not leave the Party. He was dependent for funds on Hitler. And in 1927 he was won over by being entrusted with the whole Party Organisation.

There is no space to recount here in detail the ups and downs of the inner Party history. Hitler's chief organisational task he considered to be the formation of a set of Leaders on whom he could depend. The principle of Leadership, the material dependence on him for funds, bound them to his policy. Thus he himself stated that uniformity of outlook was not important. Demagogy was encouraged. If members were won, it did not matter what the means were. The leadership remained in the hands of Hitler—and of his " patrons ". With such a policy it is not surprising that there were repeated crises among the leaders, which can be roughly summed up under two headings.

An unscrupulous policy like Hitler's inevitably encouraged leaders characterised by ruthlessness and opportunism, and some of these men made attempts to snatch the Party leadership away from their superiors. The case of Stennes, the chief of the Storm Troops of East Germany, is typical. Shortly after the electoral success of 1930, this ex-army captain began to have fears that Hitler's insistence on legal methods would fritter away the Party's advantage. He prepared a kind of inner-Party *Putsch*, whereby the S.A. would have won decisive control over the Party policy. Hitler was quicker than Stennes, however, and the unruly leader was deposed. The other type of rebel was the socialist wing of the National-Socialist Party, which believed in the 25 Points, and doubted the revolutionary sincerity of the leaders of the Party. There were innumerable examples of this type, who wavered between the National-Socialist and the Communist Party. The most notable secession was that of Otto Strasser, the brother of Gregor. With other members of the National-Socialist Party he broke away from Hitler on the grounds that the latter was betraying the lower classes. In July 1930 he founded a group with a programme in which, together with extreme nationalist views there was a violent expression of lower middle-class hatred of trustified capitalism. They were dubbed by the National-Socialists "national bolsheviks", and still have disciples, though they lost ground to Communists and National-Socialists. Finally, the case of Lieutenant Scheringer is worthy of mention. He first came before the public eye when charged, with two other army officers, with carrying on National-Socialist propaganda in the *Reichswehr*. For this he was sentenced to fortress imprisonment. On being let out on leave he demanded of the Party leaders their real intentions with regard to the Party programme, and received ambiguous, if not cynical replies. In disgust he went over to the Communists, and took an active part in combating Hitlerism.[1]

The Civil Organisation

The civil organisation of the National-Socialist Party mirrors in many ways the growth and struggles of the Party, and merits a short description. In the first period, up to 1923, the Party was dominated by the S.A., while by far the most important office of the civil organisation was Propaganda, controlled by Hitler, who had also in his hands the funds of the Party. At this time the S.A. was strongly linked up with the army and with groups of the *Freikorps*. But

[1] He pursued his Communist activities illegally through 1933 and 1934, always at the greatest risk to his life. He was killed by unknown Nazis on June 30, 1934, without trial, his body being found outside Munich.

in spite of these irregular formations, the principle of its organisation was similar to that later. The Storm Troopers were organised on an " area basis " ; their object was, as Hitler repeatedly defines it in his book, the " conquest of the streets ". Storm Troopers who lived close to one another formed the lowest unit, the *Schar*, of about 8 men ; then the *Trupp*, of about 40 ; then the *Sturm* of 100 (corresponding to the company of the regular army). These were the effectives with which other Parties were beaten off the streets, with which meetings were broken up. Bigger units embraced bigger areas. Each unit had its leader appointed, responsible to the higher commands. The whole organisation was military and intended, as its regulations stated, to train the men for action.[1] The S.S., formed in 1925, was about one-tenth of the number of the S.A. It had chiefly police functions—many of its leaders became in 1933 State police presidents. But its police functions were chiefly exercised against the S.A. The S.S. was immediately attached to Hitler and bore arms.

In 1926 the civil organisation received a new constitution, according to the new needs of the moment. Hitler, at his wits' end as to the future of the Party, and busy with his private discussions with industrialists, gave the Propaganda department to Gregor Strasser. But, by putting completely insignificant characters in the posts of treasurer and secretary he retained a vital grip on the Party. The order of importance of the Party offices is significant.

1. Propaganda (Strasser).

[1] See M. von Killinger, *Die S.A. in Wort und Bild*, 1932.

2. Finance (Schwarz).
3. Youth (undecided).
4. Sport, i.e. S.A. (Captain von Pfeffer).
5. Investigation bureau, i.e. the Party police (Heinemann).
6. Organisation (Heinemann).

Further, the following were made responsible for reports : Rosenberg for the Press ; Feder for Theoretical Finance ; Frick for Juridical matters ; A. Wagner for Trade Union questions.

No important change occurred in this order until 1930. Minor changes of personnel indicated inner Party differences—Hitler took over Propaganda from 1928 to 1930, Von Pfeffer was removed from his office. The great growth of the Party in 1930 brought about a profound rearrangement. The importance of Party action, of action in the streets and in meetings, is reflected in the advancement of Organisation to first place. Gregor Strasser, the ablest man in the Party, was appointed to control it. Propaganda moved to second place, and was given to Goebbels, the cleverest agitator. The " Sport " section, i.e. the Storm Troops, the army of the civil war, was taken over by Hitler himself, who of course still had indirect control over the Party finance. And the growing importance of the agricultural question, brought into prominence by the Crisis, is reflected in the establishment of an agricultural section, under Darré. In this year the first Agricultural Programme of the Party was published.

In 1931 an Economic section was established, under Dr. Wagener, one of whose tasks was to maintain connexions with industry. Then a section for Race and Culture, under Konopath. Very significantly the Trade Union section disappeared, and in its place a Factory Cell organisation was formed. This is a sign that, as many reports of the time tell us, the Party had hitherto failed to penetrate the working-class, and was unable to organise the proletariat on a mass basis. The method of organising, in all factories, cells of National-Socialists was now attempted. Finally, a Personal section was formed, to deal with the suitability of the many leaders. Hitler, with his hand on the funds, the Investigation Bureau, and the Personal section, retained the vital positions in the Party. His strength was shown in the contest with Strasser in 1932. Though the latter had charge then of nearly all important Party offices, including Organisation, Economics, Agriculture, Factory Cells, etc., he had none of the essential executive and financial power, and was ingloriously dismissed. After this duel Hitler broke up many of the offices, and created a special Control Commission (*politische Zentralkommission*) under his near friend Hess, as a central censorship and directive.[1]

The most prominent feature of National-Socialist organisation is the principle of Leadership. What did this principle mean in practice? It meant a complete lack of control by the Party members over their leadership. The intentions of the leaders, their political formulations, the general strategy of the Party, the origin and disposal of funds, were matters

[1] The *National-Sozialistische Jahrbücher*, 1927–33 give further information concerning these changes.

relinquished to the leaders. Often the question was raised, outside and inside the Party, "Where does the money come from?"; but Hitler did not need to give an answer. In his hands lay the whole course of the Party. We know how closely allied he was with his backers, his patrons in big industry, in the army, among the great landowners. His organisation was so formed as to allow him to steer any course that these backers might demand. The National-Socialist scorn of democracy could at any time recoil on their own heads. All their trust had to be in the Leader. They had to apotheosise him, to suggest mystical connexions between him and his movement. For there were no other ties between him and his rank and file, especially once he had stepped from Opposition to Power.

As opposed to this rigid dictatorship in the Party organisation there was astonishing irresponsibility in the Party propaganda. At different times Hitler was monarchist and republican, for the trusts and against them, etc. His lieutenants ranged from military absolutists like Göring and Epp to advocates of a working-class society like Reventlow and Strasser, from Junkers like Prince August Wilhelm to peasants. Not that these varying views were in any way coordinated. They applied to different groups, were put forward as propaganda to different classes of society. Through this many-tongued propaganda Hitler collected masses of adherents, all hoping for different results. Not until after he came to power did many of these promises show themselves as demagogy and trickery.

CHAPTER V

THE THEORY OF NATIONAL-SOCIALISM

THE theory of the National-Socialist Party is heterogeneous, undisciplined. Different times, different circumstances called forth new formulations. Profound disagreement exists between the Right and Left wings. Yet, just as there is a continuity in the Party policy and leadership, in spite of its veiled and contradictory tactics, so there is also a theory which follows this policy. Its best exponent is Alfred Rosenberg, who is to-day the official Censor of the theoretical work of the Party. If Hitler learnt from Gottfried Feder the machinations of finance, from Rosenberg he acquired the philosophical atmosphere in which his politics grew. From Rosenberg he learnt to identify Jews and Bolsheviks, international finance and Communism ; from Rosenberg he took his first lessons in foreign politics. Rosenberg, the architect, who had studied at universities, over-awed Hitler, the " water-colourist " ; his exhibition of recondite knowledge impressed the Leader, who seems to have read little but newspapers and pamphlets. In many points their main works, the *Myth of the Twentieth Century* and *My Struggle*, re-echo one another. And more important still, the body of doctrine in the *Myth of the Twentieth Century* corresponds most closely to the practical policy of the Hitler government.

All National-Socialist theory takes as its starting-point the War. An unshakable legend has been created of the unity and unquestioning loyalty of the German people during the four years of battle.[1] The breakdown of November 1919 is interpreted as an abdication to two forces, working maliciously for the destruction of Germany—international finance and bolshevism. The democratic State is the political form in which these two forces can best come to their maturity, and thus Germany was inflicted with a democratic constitution. But while these ideas were shared by the monarchist Party, the National-Socialists ruthlessly accused the age of William II as having undermined the German State, and having prepared the ground for this betrayal and collapse. They aimed not at a mere restoration of pre-War conditions, but at a rooting out of all democratic shoots and suckers from the national organism. A complete reorganisation of political life was demanded, and this necessitated a new political theory, a new political " Myth ", as Rosenberg puts it, to replace the Myth of democracy.

THE DOMINANT THEORY—ALFRED ROSENBERG

This Myth is found in the cult of the Race. The dogma of democracy centres in the freedom of the individual. Its interpretation of history would show that the political and cultural greatness of past times depends on the degree of individual liberty. Its

[1] The twentieth anniversary of the outbreak of the War, in August, 1934, was celebrated by the German government with glowing adulation of the spirit of comradeliness in the combined national effort of 1914.

avowed aim in the future is the extension of this liberty. National-Socialism challenges all the theoretical assumptions of democracy. Greatness in the past has been, it says, the result of a strong and pure race. Its aim for the future is the maintenance and purification of the Germanic Nordic race, the vital condition of future glory and strength. As a result, Rosenberg and his school turned the National-Socialist attack on Democracy into a philosophical, metaphysical assertion of opposed values. The economic or political attack was made to seem a mere consequence of the metaphysics of the movement. The advantage of this was great. It prevented National-Socialists from falling into a purely "materialistic" criticism of society, which would have led them inevitably more and more into the camp of the Communists. Faced with the alternatives of public or private ownership of banks, trusts, etc., the National-Socialists of the Left "materialistic" wing decided for the public ownership, i.e. for Socialism of some sort. But the official theory said, This is a false antithesis; the real problem is, is property in the hand of the Nordic race or of the Non-Aryans? "Socialism" is for Rosenberg the unity of a race, intent on its preservation.

Rosenberg's great service to his Party was the interpretation of the whole history of the world in terms of racial conflicts. Building largely on Houston Stewart Chamberlain, he creates, in his book the *Myth of the Twentieth Century*,[1] an extraordinary picture of the world, ranging over all times and peoples. The

[1] *Der Mythus des 20ten Jahrhunderts*, 1930.

Nordic race, the bearer of the patriarchal principle, is the only race capable of creating a political organisation of the size of the modern State, of creating a culture.[1] The Greeks were a Nordic race, and achieved their greatest political and cultural works in the period of their racial purity. When they began to mix with lesser races the creative power departed from them, their philosophy lost its purity and took on characteristics of the lower races, scepticism on the one hand, on the other Dionysiac elements, the worship of magic, of the female creative principle, of the earth, etc. Rosenberg does not take into account the inherent weakness of the Greeks, the effects of the slave-system, their scorn of manual and technical labour which spelt disaster for them. Their history is simply the history of the struggle between a Nordic race and the Non-Nordic races around it ; their fall simply the result of the " bastardising " of their blood. So also the founder of the Roman greatness, the Latin tribe, was a Nordic group. It asserted itself against the other tribes of Italy on the basis of its racial pride, and won a world dominance. Once it allowed cross-marriages between patricians and plebeians, i.e. between Nordic and other races, its decline began ; its religion changed from the proud assertion of the manlike virtues, pride, strength, loyalty, to fear,

[1] Regarding the scientific value of this conception of Race, I would refer to the statements of distinguished Non-German ethnologists, who pour ridicule both on the concept of a " pure race ", in particular of a pure " Ayran " race, and on the idea of the exclusive cultural qualities of the Aryan, Nordic race. Cf. the presidential speech of Professor Elliot Smith at the Ethnological Congress in London, July, 1934.

humility, cowardice, as embodied in superstitious rites and bloody sacrifices to monstrous gods. The Western world was reinvigorated, and Western culture rescued, by the wave of Nordic expansion from the North. Germans founded all the modern States —Spain, Italy, France, England, Germany. The Italian Renaissance is an effect of the Nordic race, its æsthetic ideal was Nordic (blonde women !), Dante was descended from German invaders.

The Nordic invasion, which flooded a decadent Rome, encountered open and hidden dams, and nowhere more powerful than in the Roman church. Rosenberg here lays the foundations of the German Christian Movement. Christ he considers an heroic personality, and consequently Nordic—a parentage is manufactured of a Roman father and a mother from the Nordic tribe of Dan. But the doctrine of suffering and love is a production of the Roman church, following the Semite Paul, and imposed on the world in order to break the Nordic supremacy. The church claim to universalism was another aspect of the attempt to sap the vitality of the Nordic race. The doctrine of original sin was wholly opposed to the pride of the Nordic nature, and could arise only in a lesser, consciously inferior breed. Thus the Roman church is shown to be the creation of inferior races. But the Aryans struggled. In particular the Huguenots fought for the Nordic principle against Rome. When they were slaughtered and driven out of France the Nordic element was destroyed in France, and only a bastard, cultureless, effete nation was left—this is Rosenberg's description of the French nation since the sixteenth century. His proof that the Huguenots were Nordic lies in the statement that the idea of freedom of belief is an "original German thought"—and that some of their leaders were blue-eyed. The Taborites and other communistic sects were however non-Nordic, both because of their doctrine and because one of their leaders, Ziska, is a Near-Asiatic type.[1] That such sects grew in Bohemia is due, says Rosenberg, to the racial characteristics of the Czechs, who are a prey to "cultureless savagery, paired with terrible superstitions". True Nordic religion must nurture Honour and Freedom, the only absolutes, "timeless and spaceless essences". And honour and freedom can be understood only in conjunction with the race; they are the forms in which man's highest service is given to the race. For the freedom of which Rosenberg and other National-Socialists speak is a national-racial freedom, a subjugation of the individual to the whole Race so that the Race shall conquer the earth. In other places Rosenberg speaks of Honour and Duty instead of Honour and Freedom. Religion consists in revering the Race and cultivating these virtues; for the mission of the Nordic race is to conquer the world and impose culture on the lesser breeds.

If, after the breakdown of the Roman Empire, the Roman Church was the bearer of the insidious

[1] There are now more cautions in Germany. The State expert for Racial Research, Gercke, declared (July 10, 1934) that physiological characteristics do not prove one's race. "One recognises race by conduct." For who among the National-Socialist leaders has the necessary long head, fair hair, and blue eyes?

Anti-Nordic bacilli, of latter times other dangerous opponents have arisen. These are the partisans of humanitarianism, democracy, socialism, carrying on the sinister struggle of the lesser races. Especially the Jews have taken the leadership in the disintegration of the Nordic race. Personally they lie in wait for the lovely Aryan maidens, besmirch their blood and weaken the Nordic race with bastards. On a larger scale they enslave the Nordic nations by the power of money. Democracy, the principle of individual liberty, frees them from restrictive control, allows them to usurp the power of States, to enslave the people. As international bankers they lay tribute on the sweat of the Nordic nations, crush them. As a second string to their bow the Jews preach the gospel of socialism. They exploit the discontent of the working-classes in order to set them against their own compatriots, to split the unity of the State. Thus the National-Socialists proclaim that socialism is a creation of the Jews, and that Socialists simply aim at delivering the world over to the rule of international finance. Hitler wrote : "The struggle of Social-Democracy against the economic life of the nation has only to prepare the ground for the rule of the really international finance and stock exchange capital." [1] Similar formulations abound in National-Socialist literature. The practical reason for this view is to be seen in the long alliance in Germany between Social-Democracy and the powers that be, in such transactions as the sale of the match monopoly to Kreuger, carried through by a Social-Democratic

[1] *Mein Kampf*, p. 234.

minister, in the honouring of the Dawes and Young Loans by Social-Democracy. More astonishing is the charge against the Communists that they also would deliver the nation to the financiers. In his edition of the *Protocols of the Elders of Zion*, a sinister forgery of the nineteenth century, in which is shown how the Jews are plotting world-revolution and anarchy, Rosenberg " reveals " the conspiracy between Soviet Russia and the centres of world-finance.[1] But apart from this, Communism attacks the Nordic principle by maintaining—by Terror, of course—a social organisation which is opposed to any cultural principle, which enslaves men, which has as its heads the Kalmuk-Tartar Lenin, the Georgian Stalin, representatives of races of destruction.

In the light of this philosophy the aim of National-Socialism is the creation of a German nation as a pure Nordic stock. The land has to be violently purged of Jews and all who suffer from their poison (Communists, Humanitarians, Pacifists). The Nordic nation, with its creed of self-assertion and conquest, will produce the great personalities which are the glory of a nation. The masses will learn that voluntary subordination which is the National-Socialist freedom. To effect these reforms a new Law will be necessary, a Law which is freed from the taint of democratic poison. The highest principle of this Law will not be an abstract Right, a respect for the individual, but the preservation of the Nordic race. The principle of punishment, says Rosenberg,

[1] Rosenberg, *Protokolle der Weisen von Zion*, 1934, p. 86 (first ed., 1923).

will be, not education nor revenge, but the delivery of the nation from racial aliens. The Law will be quite openly the political weapon of the Nordic race ; and it will not be fixed, but will adapt itself to any political situation.[1] This is the Law which the conquered enemies of National-Socialism, within and without Germany's borders, must expect.

This racial dogma is also to determine Germany's foreign policy. Rosenberg divides up the world into racial units, which are to form themselves into nations. The problem of the negro in the United States of America is solved by creating for the "niggers", as Rosenberg always calls them, a nation in Africa. The U.S.A. has simply to export its negroes to Africa, and receive in exchange white men who have settled in Africa! China will form another great racial unit and India another. The rest of the world is the space in which the great Nordic nations, England, U.S.A., and Germany will prosper. Rosenberg's audacious plan for recognising the dark and yellow races as nations is only qualified by one small condition—that the coloured races should guarantee the "rights" of the Nordic race in their territory. What this means is seen from the fact that he entirely justifies a perpetual domination of India by the British.

And what of France and Soviet Russia? These

[1] This conception of the law was precisely defined by Göring in a speech addressed to leading German lawyers, shortly after the summary execution of prominent Nazis for suspected conspiracy: "Only one conception of the Law is valid, and that is the one which the Leader himself has laid down. You (lawyers) have to act as the Law prescribes and *as the government demands of you.*" *Berliner Börsen-Zeitung*, July 13, 1934.

he recognises as the bacilli-carriers of the West. Hitler has written that Europe will not be at peace till France is colonised by Germans.[1] Rosenberg has the most hostile words for France and its culture, but more tactfully than Hitler he merely leaves her out of any future division of the world. No such scruples hold him back with regard to Soviet Russia. This " Asiatic " pest of Communism must be rooted out, the Russian nation must be thrown back beyond the line of the Urals, and Russia proper be brought back under the hegemony of the Nordic race. A preliminary step is the establishment of an autonomous Ukrainian State, under German protection. Poland, Czecho-Slovakia, and other Central European States would be reorganised, and become, to all intents and purposes, German colonies. For, says Rosenberg, these Polish, Czech, Slavonic races cannot create a nation or a culture.

It is consonant with this philosophy that economic reform takes up only a small place in the framework of racial regeneration. Too great an emphasis on economic changes would tend to materialism, the antithesis of the Nordic character. " German " socialism is simply the political organisation of the Nordic Germans. Rosenberg attacks finance and the stock exchange only in so far as they are Jewish ; he demands, not their abolition, but their restoration to the function they performed in the earlier capitalistic era, as helpmates of industry. The Corporate State is not discussed in Hitler or in Rosenberg. Private property is justified in the traditional way as

[1] *Mein Kampf*, pp. 766–7.

" solidified labour ", and these theorists refuse to analyse any further the nature of private property and the laws of capitalist economy. They are inexhaustible in their praise of capitalistic enterprise. Rosenberg suggests that in the National-Socialist State, when the democratic parliament is done away with, the economic life of the country will be controlled by the various leaders of industry, agriculture, etc. There is no question here of working-class representation, of the problem of bridging the gap between the classes of society. For Rosenberg this gap does not exist in a pure Nordic nation ; his State would make of the working-class a blind and disfranchised following, as indeed it is now become according to the Law of Nazi Germany.

There are, within the Nazi Party, many trends antagonistic to Rosenberg. But an analysis of his theory, such as is given above, is justified both by his authoritative position in the Party, and by the reality of the Party policy. Of particular significance is the fact that social reorganisation is for him merely racial reorganisation, and is carried through, not as an end in itself, as is the case with the Socialist Parties, but as a means to a political campaign of expansion and conquest. Rosenberg, like Hitler, scorns any policy which would make Germans satisfied with their present boundaries and power. He scorns plans for solving Unemployment by a policy of internal land-settlement. " To-day only one thing can help—the determined will to create territory for millions of coming Germans."[1] This is and has always been the view of the leading circles of National-Socialism.

[1] *Der Mythus des 20ten Jahrhunderts*, 1934, ed., p. 638.

Thus they combat the principle of the self-determination of nations as unleashing political and cultural disintegration.[1] They propose and hope for world-wars in the future through which the Nordic nation of Germany will gain the ascendancy over the whole world. This is the spirit which, during the War, aimed at the annexation of Belgium.

Nazi Radicals

Rosenberg, the Baltic German, the friend of Ukrainian nationalists, the rumoured friend of the oil-magnate Deterding, shaped the philosophy of the higher social circles of National-Socialism, and links on to the aristocratic nationalism of pre-War times (Treitschke, Nietzsche, H. S. Chamberlain, etc.). But National-Socialism appealed to the lower classes, attempted to win over lower middle-class and working-class. Much of the Party agitation and theory was directed towards these classes, and presents a sharp contrast to Rosenberg's and Hitler's utterances. Among the Party leaders Gottfried Feder, Count Reventlow, Gregor Strasser; among theorists Moeller van den Bruck and the periodical *Die Tat*, represent this radical tendency. Their theory, appealing to classes without social privilege and political power, suffering intensely through the Crisis, centred in a fiery attack on the economic system, on capitalism, in contrast to the cold ferocious dogmatism of Rosenberg. This type of propaganda had a wide influence on the lower classes in Germany, promising a far-reaching reform of capitalism. It has led to the

[1] Ibid., p. 648.

definition of Nazi Germany as the " State of the lower middle-class ".[1] But it must be stressed here, as it will be shown in the course of this book, that this anti-capitalistic theory was completely abandoned once Hitler came to power, and has played no part in the fashioning of present-day Germany. It is, however, of great political importance, as revealing the social situation within Germany from 1929 onwards, and as showing typical National-Socialist (we may say Fascist) methods of propaganda.

This National-Socialist group (Moeller van den Bruck, who committed suicide in 1925, was not actually a member of the Party) attacked democracy by showing up the hollowness of its pretensions. The principle of the freedom of the individual had served the few and enslaved the masses, had produced the horrors of the modern industrial system. The great democratic nations—England, U.S.A., and France—which maintained the principle of the self-determination of nations, had taken away Germany's independence and enslaved her under a financial tyranny. Democracy in Germany had acquiesced in this system, and aimed at perpetuating Germany's subjugation. It submitted to the Peace of Versailles, to Commissions of the Foreign Powers, to the Dawes and Young Agreements. It had " chased off William II in order to enthrone Parker Gilbert I ",[2] as Goebbels cried in the *Reichstag*.

[1] Calvin Hoover, *Germany enters the Third Reich* ; G. D. H. Cole, *What Marx Really Meant*, pp. 138–45 ; and numerous other publicists.

[2] Parker Gilbert was the Commissioner appointed by the Allies in 1928 to examine the state of Germany's finances.

Social-Democracy was, for this group, equally anti-German and hypocritical. They do not so much attack Socialism as being the product of a Jewish bastard race, as attempt to discredit the claims of Social Democracy to be Socialist. They point to the record of the Social-Democratic Party. In power it has been allied with big industry and finance. It has promised the socialisation of trusts and has allowed the concentration of greater and greater power and wealth in the hands of the few. It pledged the State Railways to foreign capitalists. It sold the Match Monopoly to a private industrialist, Kreuger. It claims to form an International of the working-class, but this International broke down miserably in 1914, and has scarcely the shadow of an existence. At the Hague Conference in 1929 Snowden, the representative of British Labour, screwed further millions out of Germany, whose government then contained Social-Democrats. Social-Democracy is full of the deception of a sterile movement. "The German working-class has become the sacrifice of its Marxist faith." [1] The aims of Socialism were—many of them—taken over into the programme of the radical National-Socialists. But they ridiculed Social-Democracy as an effete and treacherous instrument, become the tool of the big interests.

Many of this group differed still more from the official theorists in their attitude to the Communists and to the Soviet Union. The official Party policy towards the Communists was to terrorise them as

[1] Moeller van den Bruck, *Das Dritte Reich.*

" sub-human ", to decry them as degenerates and murderers. All responsible functionaries of the Party, no matter how radical in other matters, shared this attitude, including Strasser and Feder. But in lower circles of the Party different ideas existed. Often formal discussions were arranged between National-Socialists and Communists. Communists took part in discussions with the *Tat* circle. A public discussion was arranged between Reventlow and Communists even after Hitler came to power, though it was forbidden by the Party. And these discussions served other purposes than the discussions arranged by Goebbels in Berlin, when the Communists were prevented from speaking by organised rowdyism. The chief points of disagreement in these discussions was that the Communists were " ruled from Moscow " and not " national " enough. The National-Socialists would confess themselves " honest and thorough opponents of capitalism ",[1] but still refused to recognise the class-war. For these National-Socialist radicals the real enemy was the foreign domination ; German capitalists were to be attacked in so far as they allied themselves with the foreigners. But they claimed that the aim of national liberation was identical with the aim of the liberation of the working-classes. They admired the idea of Councils (Soviets) of workers, as realised in Russia, and demanded only a " national modification " of it.[2] Feder even proposed in the *Reichstag* a motion for the extension of

[1] Reventlow, in the *Reichswart*, June 30, 1923.

[2] Frauendorfer, *Der Ständische Gedanke im Nationalsozialismus*.

the principle of Factory Councils to all enterprises financially linked together (November 1925), though he later learned wisdom and advocated the abolition of the Factory Councils because of their "clumsiness".[1] These radicals demanded, too, the control of industry and finance by the State.

Many of their objections to Communism disappeared when they wrote of Communist Russia. They recognised that Russia through the Bolshevik revolution had broken free of the bondage of international capital. But they did not share the international policy of Communism. They interpreted the Bolshevik revolution as a national revolution, Communism they considered the political form of the Russian people. From the point of view of foreign policy they considered that Soviet Russia was the natural ally for Germany in its post-War struggle against the Allies. In 1920 Reventlow even urged a policy of military co-operation between Germany and the Soviet army then attacking Warsaw. Of later times there has been no lack of articles in the *Tat* and elsewhere advocating an alliance with Soviet Russia. There is no need to emphasise the differences here with the official outlook of the National-Socialist Party. It is sufficient to remark that the hostility towards Russia, seen in Rosenberg's and Hitler's writings, is now the official policy of Germany.

It is a remarkable and significant fact that only

[1] Gottfried Feder, *Der Deutsche Staat auf Nationaler und Sozialer Grundlage*, 12th ed., 1933. Feder is a shining example of a theoretical turn-coat.

the radical wing of the National-Socialist Party formulated a Programme and created a picture of a future Nazi State. The official Party Programme is the 25 Points, drawn up by Feder. It is a mountain conceived by a mouse. Its chief feature is the " breaking of the bondage of interest ", i.e. an attack on the strangle-hold by which the financiers choke the life out of industry and the nation. The chief measure it proposes is the nationalisation of banks and trusts. The radical wing took these Points seriously. It was in accordance with them that the plan of the Corporate State was developed. In the Corporate State, while the political organisations of the Left were to be abolished, so also were the organisations of the big interests. The State was to have complete control over all private interests. All would lose political democratic rights in order to win a due control over the productive process.[1] But it must again be stressed that these ideas embodied in the Programme and in the theory of the Corporate State never flourished in leading Party circles. In the Programme it was stated that " the leaders of the Party promise, if necessary, under the pledge of their own lives, to work ruthlessly for the carrying out of the Points ". Actually they cynically consigned them to the rubbish-heap, and to speak of them now, in Nazi Germany, is treason. And they had so fashioned the organisation of the Party that protests from underneath were impotent.

These differences between Radical Group and Party

[1] For a fuller account of the ideas of the Corporate State, see Chapter VII.

Leaders are not mere differences of opinion, they are social differences. The former spoke to and for the lower middle-class and the proletariat, the latter wrote as rulers, as the ruling class. Thus while the latter found the solution for Germany's weakness in naked, aggressive imperialism, the former aimed primarily at social reform. Many of these writers expressly denied imperialistic pretensions. Among them there grew up the ideal of " heroic abnegation ". Germany would turn its eyes from colonies and trade, and create a realm of equality and justice. In place of the conquest of Russia these writers put the ideal of " internal colonisation ". Room was to be found on Germany's own soil for the unemployed, each man would receive enough to be able to live in Spartan simplicity. To this end the great estates of the nobles, especially those that were bankrupt, would be broken up and given to the landless.[1] Similarly, the Big Stores would be made into market-places, where each little tradesman would have a stall. Enterprises which had of necessity to be carried on in large units, such as iron and steel industry, would be nationalised. Banks would serve, not oppress, the little man. Foreign Trade would be a State-monopoly. Anti-Semitic feeling was as strong among these radicals as with Hitler and Rosenberg, but was justified on social grounds. The Jews were

[1] The sharp antagonism between the two groups within the Party on this point in mirrored in the struggle over the plebiscite for the expropriation of the former Ruling Princes. Strasser's group, representing North Germany, demanded the expropriation, but was defeated by Hitler and his allies at the Bamberg Party Congress, 1926.

attacked as owners of Banks, Big Stores, etc. There was even a distinction drawn between rich and poor Jews. Goebbels, who up to 1926 belonged to the radicals, wrote, " It is probably true that the capitalist and bolshevik Jew are not one and the same thing "[1] —his sympathies being with the bolshevik Jew. This was the reverse of what Rosenberg stated, and, as Heiden says, could scarcely be called Anti-Semitism. These radicals continually used the word Socialism, meaning something very vague but all the same unpleasant for Hitler—who preferred to talk about a " national and *social* State ".

These theories of radical National-Socialism clearly betray their origin. They arose as the political creed of the German lower middle-class, as the expression of its distress. Denuded of its savings through inflation and crisis, and without hope of employment, this class had no future in the Weimar system. The Marxian analysis of history—the proletarianisation of the middle-class—was being proved true by their bitter experience. But they rebelled against it. They considered this analysis correct for the liberal, Weimar system, but believed they would establish a social order where their privileges would be preserved—an order, as they put it, in which the masses would be de-proletarianised. They shrouded themselves in a metaphysical veil, proclaiming themselves the saviours of " culture " from Communistic barbarism—they, the professional classes, architects, engineers, writers, etc., were the salt of the earth, for whom this National-Socialist revolution would take

[1] In Strasser's Fortnightly, *Nationalsozialistische Briefe*, 1925.

place.[1] So they united radical criticism of the existing regime with a radical semi-socialist programme of reform.

These men combated the materialistic interpretation of history, they refused to believe that the basis of society is its method of production, they would not accept the theory of the class-war. Their revolution would bring about, not the victory of the proletariat over the bourgeoisie, as the Communists planned, but the victory of the " socialist idea " over the idea of materialism, selfishness, class-war. But though they thought they desired a real revolution, a real ousting of the old ruling powers, they still clung fast to the " national idea ", to the hope of a national liberation. This was the rampart they threw up against Marxism, against the ideology of the proletariat. For the Germany they wished to establish, the State of Frederick the Great or of the Freiherr vom Stein, was politically and culturally the state of the middle-class. It was their indirect declaration of war on the working-class.

This is where they joined with Hitler and the powers behind him. Providing there was agreement on the question of the nation the greatest freedom was allowed in the Party theoretical writings. Only at the end of 1932 was the beginning of a Party censorship established, later to pass into the hands of Rosenberg. By their nationalism the radicals put themselves into the hands of the Junkers, of Borsig, Thyssen, Krupp, Schacht, etc. The Party organisation, its strict discipline, guaranteed the rest, guaran-

[1] Cf. Ferdinand Fried, *Das Ende des Kapitalismus.*

teed that any radical revolt could be crushed, radical demands ignored. The radicals gave the Party a mass-basis. Strasser's activity in 1932, when he put forward a radical programme as the official Programme of Action of the Party, was decisive in winning over millions for Hitler. The radical spirit infused the Storm Troops of 1932 and 1933. But it had no means of breaking loose. It was shackled to its masters. The S.A. mutinies of 1933 and 1934 were to be ingloriously suppressed. It is characteristic that leader after leader of the National-Socialist students had to be removed from office, for these radical tendencies always prospered among the students. Eventually even the last instrument of Radicalism, the Storm Troops, had to be broken. When the *condottieri* who commanded the S.A., Röhm, Ernst, Heines, etc., were killed on June 30, 1934, the last vestige of Radicalism was lost, and the S.A. became the avowed protector of the interests of the ruling class.

It is easy now, in 1934, to point out how the socialistic hopes of the National-Socialists have been cheated. It is more important to stress the role of radicalism in a Fascist movement. The same story can be told of Italian Fascism. Radical promises are made and encouraged by the leaders. Theoreticians may go to any lengths, providing the idea of the class-war is opposed. The ruling powers fear nothing but the proletariat, and the attack of the proletariat. The *Daily Herald* wrote on May 2, 1933, that the National-Socialist leaders " are bound to go forward with the 'Socialist' side of their programme ". This is an utter misrepresentation of the meaning of radical phrases—a result of the politics of the British Labour Party itself, with its refusal to accept Marxism and the theory of the class-war. Hitler himself has given us the clearest clue to his demagogy. In a phrase of *Mein Kampf*, deleted since the 12th edition (1932), he states : " The German has not the slightest notion of how a people must be misled, if the adherence of the masses is to be sought." And in his definition of the programme-maker and the politician, Hitler has no less clearly shown his hand. The programme, he says, must deal with the ideal and the *impossible* ; the politician must decide what in it is realisable, according to the objective conditions and to human powers. This lays the way open for the most absolute treachery of principle.

The theory of the National-Socialist Party is then on principle diverse and undisciplined. Its one fundamental tenet is that the class-war cannot be tolerated, that the Party which stands as the Party of the working-class must be crushed. Apart from this, everyone is encouraged to empty out his ideals and hopes on to the rubbish-heap of the National-Socialist doctrine. For ideas are not politics, not power. One cannot judge a person or a political party from its aspirations—otherwise National-Socialists, Social-Democrats, and Communists would all be very similar. Methods and actions are decisive. The radical National-Socialists did not consider that the vital antithesis in society is that between capitalist and worker, possessing and possessed.

They made a common front with the possessing against " national enemies ". They believed the " socialistic idea " would conquer. Thus they deluded themselves and the masses of their adherents. They were a necessary complement to Rosenberg and Hitler. They were the instrument of Monopoly Capital, of that Reaction about which no Party was more scornfully bitter than themselves.

CHAPTER VI

HITLER IS INDUCTED TO POWER

BRÜNING CONDUCTS DEMOCRACY FROM THE SCENE

THE history of the Crisis in Germany, the growth of the anti-democratic forces, the methods adopted to preserve the existing government machine, are an object lesson in the history of modern times. Brüning has his counterparts in the United States of America as in England. In U.S.A. and in Germany even the Social-Democrats supported the rule by presidential decree ; supported the energetic bolstering-up of capitalism by economies, subsidies, State guarantees, etc. ; endorsed the suspension of the political liberties of democracy. In England the Labour Party, faced by a similar problem, split ; some leaders went to the National Government, the Party itself abdicated before its tasks. German Social-Democracy made a permanent alliance with Brüning, even though he dropped unemployment benefits to a pitiful level, cut salaries to a minimum, sanctioned the wholesale ignoring of legal wage-contracts ; even though he entered into negotiations with the anti-democratic Right, with Hitler. Social-Democracy held fast to a regime which, while suppressing the military organisation of the Communists, looked on while Hitler's Storm Troops dominated the streets. Even industrial disputes became rare. By what means was Social-Democracy enchained to Brüning?

Brüning's policy was, in a nut-shell, to maintain German economy in the face of the avalanche of the crisis. Industry itself took protective measures—restricting production, lowering prices, etc., the results of which were increasing unemployment, wage-cuts, short-time, and so on, for the workers. The antagonism between the interests of the classes grew and threatened to take the sharpest forms, as was evident from the growth of the Communist Party. Under the leadership of the apparently "neutral" Party of the Catholics—a Party supported by powerful banking and industrial interests in the Rhine country—this yawning gulf between capitalists and employees was to be bridged. The leaders of German industry entrusted to Brüning the task of creating the political situation in which these social readjustments could be carried through. The main body which had to be reconciled with these adjustments were Social-Democracy and the Trade Unions, the leading organisations of the working-class. They were a political factor of considerable power still, especially in certain provinces of the *Reich*, such as Prussia, where they held governmental posts, with control over administration and police. Brüning's main task was then to placate the Social-Democratic Party, to persuade it of the necessities of the situation, to weld it to his policy. In this he was successful.

This would have been impossible, of course, if

Social-Democracy had disavowed capitalism. But, wedded since before the War to capitalism and the capitalist State, asserting that Socialism would grow gradually out of the democratic state, the Social-Democrats affirmed the capitalist State. Good reason told them, consequently, that the prosperity of the workers depended on the prosperity of capitalist industry. And so they acquiesced in all measures which were taken, social and economic, to ensure the health of industry. They accepted therefore the suspension of democratic rights, even the rule of Paragraph 48 ; their excuse being that it was a lesser evil than the rule of Hitlerites or Communists. Even though Paragraph 48 ruled, and the *Reichstag* met only at intervals of months, yet democratic forms were not destroyed, but only put out of operation ; of vital importance being the fact that the Social-Democratic Party itself was not destroyed, nor its members thrown out of their State offices. Thus, apparently, it only needed a governmental decision to call the old democracy back to life.

Events proved that this was a fundamental misconception. Parties are not cast-iron objects which can be disposed this way or that. They are formed of living members of social classes. If the Party consents to being put out of operation, the members do not ; and the workers began to fall away more and more rapidly from the Social-Democratic Party. The Party leadership had openly to exert all its power against working-class activities, strikes, demonstrations, etc. The rank and file were forced to remain in dull passivity, occupied, at best, with purely bureaucratic functions. What remained of Social-Democracy in 1933 was almost entirely estranged from working-class action, and collapsed miserably.

So long as Social-Democracy retained its hold on the working-class Brüning could govern Germany. But there was a further problem, of great urgency. This was the vast unrest in circles outside the orbit of Social-Democracy, amongst the lower middle-class so hard hit by the crisis. These masses demanded radical social changes, not the slow, cautious adjustments of Brüning. Many of them voted for Hitler and were organised in the Storm Troops. So long as these masses remained with Hitler, they could be used, directly or indirectly, to enforce the anti-working-class policy of the Brüning government. As a military factor they had far less importance than is usually ascribed to them ; even when thirteen millions voted for Hitler, Von Papen could override them with equanimity. What was, however, the key to the existence of the Brüning government was, how far and how long he could prevent these National-Socialist followers from leaving Hitler and going over to the Communists. If the working-class threw off the control of Social-Democracy, if the semi-proletarianised middle-class slipped away from the leadership of Hitler, then the social revolution was in sight. If Brüning allowed this, he would be displaced by a completely dictatorial government.

It seems that Brüning himself, and his circle of advisors, realised this ; certainly Hindenburg and his group followed a programme based on similar calculations. During the years of the rule of Paragraph

48 opinion was weaned from the idea of democracy. Social-Democracy lost its power as an organ of struggle, on the political and industrial field. On the other hand, the Parties of the Right were brought closer together. Largely through the good offices of Thyssen, Hitler came into close contact with the leading industrialists of Germany, adapted his tactics more to their needs, received their support. In certain provincial governments—in Thuringia and Brunswick—the National-Socialists gained practical experience of the problems of the reconstruction of capitalism. In 1931 the two Parties, National-Socialists and Nationalists, formed the so-called Harzburg Front, an alliance to overthrow Brüning with his allies the Social-Democrats. Though this alliance was fragile, it was symptomatic of the concurrence of interest between the " revolutionary-conservative " forces of the Nazis and the frank reaction of the Party of Hugenberg. Brüning also, though still enjoying the confidence of Social-Democracy, entered into negotiations with Hitler, asking for his support on the Reparations question, promising as *quid pro quo* the Chancellorship to Hitler, once the Reparations question was settled (January 1932).

In other ways, too, Hitler's cause was furthered. Demonstrations of Nazis were allowed, under police protection, to march provocatorily through working-class districts, before Socialist and Communist headquarters ; if resistance was shown, the police punished it severely. In the Spring of 1932 the Nazis broke into the building of *Vorwärts*, the Socialist newspaper, and paraded before it for hours afterwards, without action being taken by the (Social-Democratic) police. It is characteristic of Social-Democracy that it too, like Brüning, faced with the alternatives of revolutionary or reactionary policy, began to prepare for the advent of the National-Socialists to power. In the Spring of 1932 Severing, who was so much lauded as the leader of the Anti-Fascist Movement of Social-Democracy, wrote, " Now both Centre and Social-Democratic Parties have the wish to give the National-Socialists the opportunity of testing their promises against hard facts ", i.e. to give the Nazis a share in the government !

Though under Brüning Germany was clearly driving towards a more nationalist, more anti-working-class form of social organisation, there were differences in ruling circles as to the rate of development. The crisis was deepening rapidly. After the smash of the *Danat Bank* and the wool combine, *Nordwolle*, in 1931, allied banks and industries were in a desperate plight. The Steel Trust itself was threatened with bankruptcy, and with it would be broken the backbone of German capitalism. Clearly desperate remedies were necessary. The main problem was, how much opposition would the working-class oppose to these remedies ; could they be administered within the framework of the Constitution, which allowed rights of organisation and opposition to the working-class, or was a new organisation of society necessary ? It was no accident that the Catholic Party accepted the nominal leadership in this reorganisation, since its control over the working-class would be seriously weakened under a regime openly tyrannous to the working-class. It was natural, too, that the Centre should receive the support of that part of industry not yet monopolistic, which hoped still for a revival of the times of free competition, once the crisis was overcome. Monopolistic industry, however, and agriculture went over more and more completely to Hitler-Hugenberg, setting its only hope in the absolute and thorough crushing of all organisations which could check the revival of German industry.

The Presidential Elections of the Spring of 1932 showed the trend of opinion, especially when taken in conjunction with Brüning's negotiations with Hitler in January. The democratic Parties had Hindenburg as their candidate, reversing the position of seven years before, when in the eyes of Social-Democracy he had been the personification of Reaction. From the Left he was opposed only by Thälmann, the Communist leader. But from the Right he had against him not only Hitler, as National-Socialist candidate, but also Colonel Duesterberg, the Nationalist. The result was that Hindenburg did not win the necessary absolute majority on the first ballot, and on the second gained only 4 million votes more than Hitler—19·3 millions to Hitler's 13·4. Many of Duesterberg's supporters voted on the second ballot, when the Nationalist candidate had retired, for Hitler. Thälmann received 5 million votes on the first ballot, and 4 millions on the second. Thus Hindenburg, through his support of the Brüning regime, was isolating himself from his former friends and associates, and allying himself with Social-Democracy. Soon, however, he was to see that this alliance must be broken. The high-water mark of his trust in Brüning was the dissolution of the Storm Troops, decreed in April 1932, but even this was only a paper-decree, not thoroughly carried out.

The effect of Brüning's policy was not merely the strengthening of the Reaction ; the radicalisation of the masses also proceeded apace. The militant workers were showing a tendency towards the Communist Party. And in National-Socialist circles radical tendencies were spreading. In 1932 the most powerful personality in the Hitlerite party was Gregor Strasser. He it was who, in May of this year, formulated the phrase " anti-capitalistic yearning " as characteristic of the German masses. He threw out feelers in the direction of the Trade Unions. This was the contingency dreaded by the government. Brüning attempted to ban this evil spirit of the union of radical forces by making concessions to the masses. Since the beginning of the crisis prices of agricultural products had been maintained by the various governments, by Social-Democrats as by Brüning. Now, in 1932, prices began to fall. Rents were re-valuated at a lower level. Landlords and Junkers were hit worst. Then Brüning planned his boldest step. He made preparations to break up the heavily indebted estates of the Prussian Junkers, in order to provide land for the settlement of the unemployed. His compensatory measure, the compulsory lowering of interest rates on loans to agriculture, did not relieve the land much, and alienated the bankers.

This was Brüning's first step against the possessing classes, and their toleration was immediately withdrawn from him. The plan touched Hindenburg himself very nearly. In 1927 this Grand Old Man of the Republic had been presented by the *Reich* Federation of Industry with an estate in Prussia, Neudeck, and thus had become one of the largest landowners in Germany. Neudeck became his constant residence. Here he lived surrounded by his personal friends, by his neighbours, former officers and landowners like himself. For the sake of landowners such as these Brüning had introduced the notorious *Osthilfe*, a subsidy directed to the maintenance of agriculture in East Prussia, which had been largely absorbed by the large landowners. But these large estates were in the end too big a burden for Brüning. He planned to disembarrass them by breaking them up partially, and to relieve unemployment by devoting the land thus acquired by the State to a settlement-policy; a plan which had been much discussed in radical circles of the Right as well as of the Left. This was too much for Hindenburg, who would have finally lost all his friends and allies by sanctioning such a plan. Hindenburg's faithfulness to his class reasserted itself, and he withdrew his confidence from Brüning in a curt interview which filled the latter with bitter disillusionment.

Open Reaction—von Papen

With the departure of Brüning the *Reichstag* lost every vestige of authority. Hindenburg nominated von Papen to the Chancellorship, a Catholic member of the Nationalist Party, and member of the *Herrenklub* (the Gentlemen's Club), an exclusive club from which he chose most of the members of his cabinet and to which von Schleicher, the Chief of the *Reichswehr*, also belonged. Here was an authoritarian government indeed, without any mass following. Intrigue and accommodation were its methods, based on the authority of the President and the strength of the *Reichswehr*.[1]

Von Papen's first aim was to acquire a position of power where it was most easily accessible. The control of the Prussian administrative apparatus, in particular of the Prussian police, was his first objective, and the attack was directed against the Prussian Socialists, who were in charge of the Prussian Ministry of the Interior. To do this Papen made a bargain with the Nazis. He annulled the ban on the S.A. and S.S., who now reappeared in resplendent new uniforms ; he promised Hitler new elections. As a direct result of this pact can be considered the provocatory demonstration of uniformed Storm Troopers through the working-class district of Altona in Hamburg. Even official circles were reluctant to allow this. When carried through—under heavy police protection—an open struggle took place between workers and Nazis, with several dead and wounded on both sides. A further penalty of blood was exacted in 1933, when Communist workers were sentenced to execution by Hitler's judges for their part in resisting this provocation. On this basis Papen won Hitler's temporary neutrality. Then he went forward to his attack. On July 20 he abolished

[1] A fairly detailed account of the intrigues of this period is contained in Konrad Heiden, *Geburt des dritten Reiches*, 1933.

the constitutionally elected government of Prussia—a coalition of Social-Democracy and Catholic Centre—and replaced it by a Commissar responsible to Hindenburg and the Papen government. Braun and Severing, the Socialist leaders, said that only force could remove them. A lieutenant and a corporal's guard were sufficient.

If the Reaction in Germany needed moral encouragement, then it was provided by the effete collapse of German Social-Democracy in face of this impudent provocation of the representatives of the working-class. The legal government of Prussia was ousted on the basis of Paragraph 48, the reasons given were that this government had not been energetic enough against the Communists and had no popular support—it was ironical to hear the latter reason from Papen, of all men. The Communists appealed to the Social-Democrats to unite in a General Strike, the only possible answer to such an open breach of the Constitution. With the Prussian police still under Socialist influence and leadership the strike might well have been successful. But the Socialist leaders showed how their principles and vitality had been sapped by their years of collaboration with the Republic. They turned to the Right to justify themselves, instead of to the Left to defend the working-class. Only the day before the *Coup* Severing had written in the *B.Z. am Mittag* that political action by the Prussian police had caused more victims on the Left than on the Right. Now they refused to oppose von Papen; and, to save their faces, they appealed to the Supreme Court of

Law at Leipzig, and said they would decide what action should be taken after the legal judgment had been given. This must be considered as one of the master-strokes of political ineptitude—or treachery to the working-class—that the modern world has seen. The verdict of the Supreme Court, given on October 25, was typical of post-War German justice. It stated that the Coalition government of Prussia was still the legal government, but that since the President had considered it necessary to nominate a Commissar, this must be a legal act. The executive power must therefore be in Papen's hands, and the "sovereignty" in the hands of the former government. What this legal blarney meant was, that the *status quo* must be recognised, political factors being stronger than legal. But whatever the verdict might have been, the postponement of action until after a court of law had considered Papen's *coup d'état* was political suicide. It was the legitimate heir of the Social-Democratic policy in 1918 and 1919. By the time the judgment was given the whole administrative apparatus of Prussia and the police force was under the control of the reactionaries.[1]

Von Papen had struck shrewdly, for he had struck that opposition Party which held the position of greatest advantage and was least able to defend

[1] One is forcibly reminded of the legalistic, unpolitical decisions of the General Council of the T.U.C., and the Labour Party Executive with regard to the proposals of the Communist Party, or even of Sir Stafford Cripps for taking steps towards the establishment of Socialism in England. Austrian Social-Democracy, too, followed this line until all strategic positions had been lost.

itself. But a hornets' nest was stirred up by his concessions to the Nazis, and the Communists were rapidly taking the place of Social-Democracy as the chief organisation of the working-class. Towards the Communists Papen took the sharpest measures, banning their newspapers, imprisoning their leaders, forbidding them all rights. With the National-Socialist Party he played a dangerous game, which was justified on the whole, though it has turned out otherwise than he expected. His Party had no wish to submit to the will of the masses, " inexpert " in the conduct of politics and industry. Through discussions with Hitler and other Nazi leaders he was convinced, firstly, that he could lead them by the nose, and, secondly, that their revolutionary demagogy was intended to mislead the masses, and would be discarded when they were given a share in the government. This judgment, though right in essence, was wrong in that it characteristically failed to estimate correctly the surging passions of the masses, and their urgent demands for changes in society and outlook.

Tempting as it is to describe the events of 1932 in terms of the political scheming of the heads of the various Parties, the real characteristic of the year is the mass-feeling which urged these Parties one way or the other. Scarcely a single person was left untouched by the political issues of the day. The crisis had bitten deep into the people. Unemployment, the anxiety concerning food, clothing and shelter, touched all sections of the people. At elections over 90 per cent of the electorate would vote. The Nazis, by far the largest Party, spoke to the masses in terms they could understand, in terms of action, mass action. The Storm Troops, now as in 1923 the centre of the party life, were organised for action, with military discipline and a prescribed sphere of activity. They appealed to a desperate people with promises of clearing away the old authorities, the old system. They raised the spirits of an oppressed middle-class by spectacular processions, with waving blood-red swastika banners—Hitler himself had chosen blood-red as their colour; under the protection of the police they carried out provocatory demonstrations through the working-class, Communist quarters of the great cities, showing how might could silence and browbeat the "red terror".

There was a mass revolt against the liberalistic age. Concretely this revolt resulted in constant civil warfare with the Communists. Because of this the adherents of the middle-classes flocked to the National-Socialist Party. But at the same time it was repeated over and over again that there was no longer a middle-class in Germany. Savings had been depleted through the inflation, and the crisis had done the rest; the middle-class which flocked to the Nazis had lost much of its privilege of security and wealth. And so its oppression of the Communists was shot through with desires for a new age. In an imposing speech in the *Reichstag* on May 10 Gregor Strasser expressed the "yearning" of the people for a state which would no longer think in terms of dividends, world-economy, export figures, but would concern itself primarily with providing a decent reward for honest work.[1] So practical and sensible a demand found an echo in many hearts. Strasser even entered into negotiations with the leaders of the Trade Unions, who had for some time been growing dissatisfied with the Social-Democratic policy. In an important speech in October to the factory organisations of the National-Socialist Party Strasser actually mentioned with approval the name of the president of the Trade Union Congress, Leipart.

The masses demanded a concrete plan of recovery from their distress. Authoritative programmes of the Nazi Party answered this demand. Feder published in the official Party organ, the *Völkischer Beobachter* of April 2, proposals for giving work to half a million unemployed through the Labour Service, and to another half-million through a slight rearrangement of the house tax. With the greatest confidence he proclaimed that these measures needed only a stroke of the pen, once the old system, the old " Marxistic-Liberalistic " apparatus was swept away. Above all a programme of Strasser's summed up the hopes of the rank and file of the Party. As leader of the Organisation of the Party he formulated a programme in July 1932 which was to serve as a basis for the election propaganda of the Party speakers for the elections of July 31. It is expressly stated in this pamphlet that other views are to be considered private opinions, and do not correspond to the party outlook.

[1] This speech was considered representative enough to be printed as a pamphlet under the title " Work and Bread ".

The main lines of this programme are as follows:[1] The chief need at the moment is the conquest of impoverishment, and the method is to create work —" not capital creates work, but work creates capital ". It is a capitalist lie that over-production exists. Germany has not enough. All that is needed is to turn away from the foreign market, which is exhausted, and create an internal market through the establishment of public works of all sorts. The chief cost of work schemes is wages, and through the sealing of Germany from imports these costs will flow back to the people in one form or another. The necessary capital for these schemes can be found by the State through " the productive creation of credit " (cf. Feder's credit schemes, pp. 78–80). The interest on foreign debts—reckoned in 1932 at 22 milliards of marks—must be lowered, and a moratorium granted on short-term loans. In order to compete on the foreign market Germany must leave the gold-standard. Rates of interest within the country must be lowered—Brüning's example has shown that this can be done; in order to ensure success the banks must be nationalised. Those industrial monopolies which are not dismembered must be nationalised, and joint stock companies placed under State control. The land must be developed so as to employ a million more land-workers and to make Germany self-sufficient; 400,000 small houses are to be erected, giving work to a million men.

[1] *Wirtschaftliches Sofortprogramm der N.S.D.A.P.*, July 1932 (Economic Programme of Immediate Action).

One scarcely knows at which aspect of this programme to wonder more, at its socialistic aspect—for it is based on the Marxist tenet that labour produces wealth—or at its unscrupulousness. Its statistics are false, its finance phantastic; altogether it promises immediate work for three or four millions of unemployed. But it had an enormous success, selling half a million copies, and it was the banner under which the Hitlerites marched to their greatest electoral success. The results of the July elections were, that the Nazis polled nearly 14 million votes and won 230 seats in the *Reichstag*. Papen had reckoned without his host. His own party had a miserable 40 seats. The Social-Democrats suffered also, dropping to 133 seats and 7 million votes; but the Communists were growing, and with 4 million votes won 89 seats in the *Reichstag*.

The position was serious for the government. At first attempts were made to harness the seething masses of the Nazis to the existing system by taking Hitler into the government in the subordinate position of Vice-Chancellor. The negotiations broke down. The political combination behind Papen—big landowners and industrialists—then set about a plan of retrenchment of their own, ignoring the desperation in the country. It was not easy to satisfy all members of the cabinet. For the agriculturists a protective policy was engaged on, surpassing by far the measures of Brüning. A system of import-quotas was established, so as to secure the internal market for German produce at whatever cost. The result was a big increase of prices, which estranged the industrialists as it caused the cost of living for their employees to rise. For the employers Papen endorsed a wide campaign of wage-cuts. The Free Trade Unions were more and more ignored, and the Company Union favoured. To absorb unemployment the Labour Service was developed, and by the end of November 300,000 men were employed in the labour camps, at a cost per man of 600 marks yearly to the State. It was clear that these measures were not in themselves a solution of the crisis ; but there was a faint improvement to be noticed in these months, production increased, and the seasonal Christmas business swelled the volume of trade. Papen himself was fond of dabbling in foreign politics, and here he reaped the fruits of Brüning's policy—a final settlement of Reparations in August 1932, at the sum of 3 milliards of marks.

Papen was successful in stemming the flood of the Nazi movement. But the waters trickled over the banks and began to flow to join another stream. Social-Democracy was obliterated as a militant political force ; the Trade Unions acquiesced in the wage-cuts. But violent resentment broke out among the workers who suffered from Papen's industrial and agricultural policy, and a series of strikes broke out all over the country, surpassing in bitterness and determination any since 1923. And these strikes were under Communist influence and leadership, directed against all the framework of society, from Papen's government to the Trade Union leadership. Some ot these strikes, different from the majority in the years 1930 and 1931, were successful, and a vigorous spirit spread through the ranks of the working-class. The culmination of this movement was the Berlin Transport strike of the beginning of November, declared at the very time of the *Reichstag* elections. Wage-cuts had been announced, and the workers, despite the advice of the Trade Union leaders, decided to struggle. Communists led the strike, which brought about an almost complete stoppage of Berlin traffic for several days. The most energetic measures were adopted by the workers, which were countered by violent measures by the State. " Scab " vehicles were overturned and stoned, scab workers injured. The police retaliated by imprisoning all the ring-leaders wherever they could be found. It was not a struggle between men and employers, but between men and the State, and the Trade Union leaders fought openly against the strikers. The strike was broken by the use of the whole weight of the authority of the State, and the militant workers were not reinstated. But the strike was a sign of the times, not to be misread by those in power.

In the elections of November 6 Papen's own Party gained somewhat, and the National-Socialists lost 2 million votes. In this the government's tactics were successful. But where had these lost votes gone? Some no doubt to Papen. But National-Socialists had openly joined in the Berlin Transport strike. The Nazi leaders had had to avow this, saying rather shamefacedly that they supported the strike in order not to discredit their Party in the eyes of the proletariat.[1] This was where Papen's openly reactionary policy was bringing the masses. His talk of changing the Constitution, of introducing a Second Chamber of Privilege, aggravated this tendency. His policy was solidifying the revolutionary forces within the proletariat, and fusing with them the followers of Hitler. In these elections of November, the last free elections of Germany, the Communists polled 6 million votes, and won 100 seats in the *Reichstag*, nearly reaching the numbers of Social-Democracy. Underneath all the trumpetings of the various parties there sounded the alarm : if the Communists are growing like this there will be a proletarian revolution.

The Nationalist Party, the naked rule of big interests, could not provide an outlet for the desperate masses. If Hitler's Party were not given free rein, Hitler's followers would go with the Communists, as they had done in the Transport Strike. Papen's cunning was obstinate blundering, for he was frittering away the Nationalist *élan.* The powers behind Hitler—Thyssen, the Big Industrialist, and his like—began to act. They sowed disruption in Papen's cabinet. Schleicher said that if civil war broke out he could not rely on the army. When Papen went to Hindenburg to ask him for powers to carry on the Presidial government, Hindenburg refused him his confidence.

[1] Cf. Goebbels, *Vom Kaiserhof zur Reichskanzlei*, p. 191 : "If we had withdrawn from this strike our firm footing among the working-men would have been shaken."

HITLER IS INDUCTED TO POWER

The Army and the Trade Unions—or Hitler?

Hitler, the leader of the mass-party, was offered the Chancellorship under certain conditions. He refused. After days of agitated negotiation between the various interests Schleicher, whose executive was his army, was appointed Chancellor, as the man representative of Big Industry. He immediately abolished Papen's import quotas, and pursued a more conciliatory policy towards the Trade Union leaders. He also set in motion certain schemes of public works—he was faced with an Unemployment figure of 6 million registered unemployed, and at least 2 million unregistered. At the same time he and his backers recognised the need for giving the National-Socialists a share in the government. He entered into negotiations with Hitler through the medium of Strasser. Here the latter's old connexions with the Trade Union leaders were doubtless to play their part. Schleicher was never clear as to his plans, but it seems that he hoped to conciliate the working-class by making an alliance with the Trade Union leaders. Hitler broke off the negotiations, as he would not accept this alliance. Strasser, however, conducted them secretly further. He proposed to join up with Schleicher, carrying over with him from the National-Socialist Party a section of the more socialistically inclined. But the plot was discovered. At a tearful meeting of the leaders of the Party Strasser's plans were revealed and he was sent on leave, losing his offices. His former sympathisers deserted him, returning to the fold. The lesson of the Party crisis was, that National-Socialism would make no pact with working-class organisations.

But, for the Nationalist Parties, the situation was threatening. Hitler had lost votes in the November elections, and now his own leaders were splitting away from him.[1] The general opinion was that he had missed his opportunity and his Party would disintegrate. The Nationalist leaders were aware of this, and knew that the only gainers would be the Communists. And so, on January 4, Papen met Hitler, bitter foes since August, but now wiser. The landowners had withdrawn their support from Schleicher, and he, in return, had instituted a commission to investigate the administration of the *Osthilfe.* It was rumoured that the big landed interests had appropriated the fund to their private advantage. The matter threatened to turn into as bad a scandal as the Barmat affair, and prompt action was needed to hush it up. Papen was in a hurry to negotiate with Hitler, and was not too anxious, perhaps, about the terms, since he thought he was dealing with the leader of a diminishing Party. It did not help Hitler particularly that he scored a success in the elections of the smallest German State, Lippe-Detmold. And so a bargain was struck. When Schleicher went to Hindenburg to ask for powers to dissolve the *Reichstag* if it refused him a vote of confidence, Hindenburg turned down the general as abruptly as he had turned down Brüning.

[1] A lively impression of the despair at that time in the National-Socialist Party is given by Goebbels in his diary, *Vom Kaiserhof zur Reichskanzlei.* Hitler contemplated suicide. The situation is spoken of as " catastrophic ".

Rumours of the army's marching on Berlin circulated; but for what were they to establish a military dictatorship? The forces of wealth and privilege had played long enough with government over the heads of the masses. They realised at last that they must turn to the masses, must adopt a demagogic voice. Papen and Hitler formed a government with Hitler as Chancellor, Papen as Vice-Chancellor. Members of the Nationalist Party filled most of the Ministerial posts. Hugenberg had the Ministries of Economics and Agriculture; von Neurath was Foreign Minister; Seldte, the leader of the Steel Helmets, became Minister of Labour. But Hitler was entrusted with those posts where closest contact with the masses was needed. Frick was made Minister of the Interior. Göring became Prussian Minister of the Interior. In Papen's view, these men were to transform the policy of the government into the language acceptable to the masses; they were to create the organisational forms necessary to re-establish German economic life. These functions they have carried out. But from Hitler's point of view, from the point of view of the National-Socialist Party, these Ministries were also the strategic positions in the government. They gave Hitler all power in the State. The police was in his control; he had the auxiliary weapon of the Storm Troops, who only needed arms to carry through his orders. It is true that Hitler assured the world of his "Constitutional" intentions; but while his allies only controlled the direction of his attack, he had the power to direct the tactics himself, and, if need be, to oust any rival colleagues.

CHAPTER VII

THE VISION OF THE CORPORATE STATE

It is as well to pause in the historical account here, at the moment of Hitler's accession to power, and to try and picture what expectations were dominant among the mass of his supporters who marched in an endless troop past the window in the *Wilhelmstrasse* where their Leader received their homage. All felt a great destiny hovering near. The ups and downs of the negotiations with Papen and the reactionary interests had injured Hitler's reputation and lost him supporters, temporarily; the actual governmental alliance gave cause for concern. But Hitler had been explicit in his book about the tortuous methods of the politician. He had come to power, no matter by what means. He had behind him the organised masses of his Storm Troops, two or three hundred thousand of them. They were waiting for his programme, for his command.

The masses of the Nazi Party confidently expected a thorough social reform, to spring out of the first step, the abolition of political Parties and parliamentary government. Hitler had lost votes at the end of 1932 because of his seeming faithlessness to the radical points of his Programme. Now the masses rallied to him, believing that mass support would enable him to beat down reactionary interests.

The publications of the radical wing of the National-Socialists were printed in edition after edition in 1932 and the first half of 1933. Feder assured the German people, and with emphasis, that the Leaders of the Party still held by the 25 Points, still promised to realise them, "if necessary at the risk of their lives". The Programme, he proclaimed, must be "a true reflection of the coming State and economic system".[1] True it was over-hasty, or rather incorrect, to assume, as did Hans Zehrer of *Die Tat*, that the creation of the new State would imply the abdication of the political Party of the Nazis in favour of a new social order, the "de-politicising of Germany", the "neutral" State. But it was widely believed that the National-Socialist Party would, while ridding itself of its reactionary allies, build up around it a social order which would remove the productive workers of the State from political preoccupations and set them in a world where the old political arguments would be eliminated. This yearning for a new society penetrated into circles which had formerly been closed to any thought of social reform. Nearly all the German periodicals of 1933 have their articles on the Corporate State, very vague and confused as a rule and unconversant with the reality of the political forces involved, but a striking testimony to the general expectations in the people.

Public Interest before Private Interest

National unity was the driving force of the construction of the National-Socialist State: this was

[1] Feder, *Der deutsche Staat auf nationaler und sozialer Grundlage*, 12th edition, 1933, p. 40.

the principle which was to heal the divergences of the class-State, to eradicate Marxism, the definition of the class-State. At the opposite extreme from the Marxist, the National-Socialist conception of the State is that of a " community with one culture and one destiny ", of a " national race bound by ties of blood and fate ".[1] This combination of racialism with nationalism implied the elimination of foreign elements from all leading posts in the State, i.e. of the Jews. Religion would be set to its service— " suppression of all religious creeds which are antagonistic to the German feeling of morality and bear a content destructive of State and People ".[2] " Public Interest before Private Interest " is the main slogan of National-Socialism, and is directed chiefly against the private interests of certain classes within the State. " The National Existence in its most comprehensive form is the true wealth of a nation ", as Adam Müller had answered Adam Smith in the early nineteenth century. The ideal example of this service to the nation is for Hitler and his Party the year of service in the army of pre-War Germany, or the year in the Labour Service, when every member of the State gives himself and his labour to the State on equal conditions, demanding no return for this service.

The radical theoreticians of the National-Socialist Party considered their conception of the State to differ essentially from any other modern conceptions.

[1] Hans Buchner, *Grundriss einer nationalsozialistischen Volkswirtschaftstheorie*, p. 7.

[2] Feder, *op. cit.*, pp. 44.

Obviously the liberal state is different. The theory that greater and greater individual liberty is compatible with the preservation of national life is strongly combated by the Nazis. They point to the havoc wrought in economic life by this principle of freedom, to the disintegration in political life, the rise of Marxist parties caused by this refusal to accept the State as the norm of our existence.[4] But radical Nazi opinion distinguished the Nazi State strongly from that of pre-War or " reactionary " nationalism. While accepting the stock German definition, " State is Power ", they interpreted power as inward not outward power. They repudiated the desire for expansion and dominion of foreign races. Their militarism, which they say arises from the need for maintaining the hegemony of the State over all particular interests, is not to be directed against foreign countries, but is merely a school of discipline, of renunciation of selfish morality. Thus their economic principle is not profit-seeking and expansion of trade, but *Bedarfsdeckung*, the covering of need, not a selfish but a communal aim. Their political principle is " autarchy ", national self-sufficiency, the sealing off of their state from international competition and complications. That these aims serve militaristic ends is evident. In the last war the dependence of Germany on imports contributed largely to her defeat. But this striving for autarchy is attributed by the National-Socialist theoreticians to

[1] Parallel ideas in England were expressed in the broadcast speech of Walter Elliot, the present Minister of Agriculture, April 1934.

a moral, not a military, motive. In place of capitalistic materialism, which schemes for the enrichment of the possessing; in place of Marxist materialism, which aims at the prosperity and self-government of the masses, they put a "heroic" self-denying idealism. True culture, moral and æsthetic, they say, arises from a racially pure, strong State. No sacrifice is too great to ensure this strength. The State must be strong and united enough to maintain itself against the attacks of foreign nations—Reparations and foreign debts are continually in the minds of the Nazis—but must also be strong enough to control trade with foreign lands.[1]

Banking Capital and Industrial Capital

In this connexion many National-Socialist writers make use of Feder's famous distinction between creative and rapacious capital. Capitalism grew to its finest blossom under the influence of the creative spirit, which inspired men to produce manifold varieties of goods. Capital in its "natural" form was the reward of this spirit, not the condition of its success; it is this spirit in its pristine purity which urges every German grocer, butcher, confectioner to produce new and delightful variations of sausages and sweets. Among the great examples of the creatively inspired Feder quotes the German captains of industry—Krupp, Mannesmann, Thyssen, Siemens, Borsig, Krauss, Maffei—all men, as he says, whose

[1] It is to be noted that these views are those of a certain section of Nazi writers whose influence was wide-spread in the masses at this time. Hitler himself has since denounced these "petty unambitious ideals".

aim was " not their own gain, but the prosperity of their works ". The rapacious spirit moves the banks, finance-capital, above all the Jews, to a lesser extent all shareholders who are not engaged in the productive process. The banks prosper merely by lending out money and waiting for the interest to fall due. The crassest example is to be found in international finance-capital—money is the international power *par excellence*—which sucks out a country's blood without contributing to its welfare. Feder and his like ignore the fact of the decreasing power and independence of the banks, just as they ignore the organic function of bank-finance in capitalism. The increase in the size of concerns, the need for capital in vast quantities in heavy industry, which has to be established in huge units, makes banking operations on a large scale necessary ; since the War, particularly, heavy industry has had greater and greater control over the German banks. Feder's aim is to free industrial enterprise from the control of the outsiders, the banks, a control they acquire through being large shareholders. Freed from this dead hand, the manager of the enterprise can pursue a " creative " policy, can become once again the " leader " of his works.

Feder is intrepid in his speculation as to how to capitalise big projects and bridle the power of the banks. In spite of the lively horror in Germany of inflation he does not shrink from recommending it. If the State is the supreme monetary power, why should it not simply print more money in order to capitalise new schemes of construction ? An essential point is the breaking of the slavery of interest, and Feder has several schemes for the capitalisation of public works without interest. The favourite one is the establishment of special banks for building and industrial projects. These would finance any given undertaking by issuing " shares " without interest, which would be guaranteed by the State and covered by the productive value of the undertaking once it was working. The shares would be issued in the form of special " share " money, to be redeemable within a given period of years—a species of inflation in which the extra money in circulation is supposed to be covered by the productive value of the schemes engaged upon. In this way the " bondage of interest " would be broken; and State control would be affirmed exactly where it was needed, i.e. where private enterprise showed itself ineffective.

However, strong as the national interest in the economic life of the nation must be, the Nazis do not favour wholesale nationalisation of industry. Even in the radical Feder we find that Point 13 of the Party Programme—" We demand the nationalisation of the concerns so far trustified "—has turned in his 1933 programme to " Gigantic concerns are to be opposed ". The national interest demands a " healthy and independent economic system ", ensuring creative enterprise. Nationalisation must be subordinated to this. And so Feder recommends only the nationalisation of the banks, of transport, and of commerce. And even here, while the two former are to be under direct State-control (Feder admires the State railway system as a model), commerce is to be controlled only indirectly by a system of tariffs, quotas, import boards, and subsidies. The realm of production and consumption is the real sphere of private enterprise. Cartels and trusts are to be disbanded in the interests of the creative spirit of competition, though Feder recognises that certain types of industry need to be organised on a large scale.

The Corporate State

There seems to hover before the eyes of these Nazi theoreticians a certain ideal harmony in economic life, a harmonious proportion between big, little, and medium-sized enterprises. Buchner, indeed, tries to establish this scientifically as far as agriculture goes. He analyses the development of agriculture and comes to the conclusion that the market for agricultural produce is an economic constant which has a vital bearing on the development of agricultural economy. As a concrete result he states that agricultural concerns, instead of following the law of capital accumulation laid down by Marx, do not increase in size. In fact, he attempts to show that the number of small farms and peasant holdings in Germany is greater now (1933) than before the War, and the large estates are less able to hold their own under conditions of capitalist competition. The chief reason for this is the national policy of capitalist States, which aims at preserving its agriculture and protecting it against the foreign producer, a policy which Marx, so he says, did not foresee.[1] It is on the basis of this defined market—the national market—that a harmony in economic relationships is posited by the theorists of the Corporate State. Economic development here will be " organic ", i.e. will not disturb this relationship. Of course there is in this theory a sublime obliviousness to the fact that German industry has been built up essentially with a view to the foreign market, and that immense and uncontrollable distress would follow on an autarchist plan of these dimensions. Hitler, Thyssen, Schacht, and the other responsible leaders have never been misled by such plans. To the masses they represented a short and attractive method of release from Germany's problems.

The Corporate State itself is to be built up on the basis of this harmony of economic relationships within capitalism. Buchner puts it concisely—a certain relationship between market and production, based on the " spatially defined organism of an economic entity ", i.e. on the State as it is geographically and politically defined, determines the Corporate State. Two main changes are necessary : firstly, to break down anti-State political organisations and feelings ; secondly, to build up in each man the feeling of responsibility for his job, to make it possible for each man to participate actively in the control of his own work. Under liberalistic capitalism the working-

[1] Hans Buchner, *op. cit.*, pp. 32–3. Buchner does not take into account that first the War, then the Inflation, provided agriculture with a temporary stabilisation, nor does he mention the growing crisis in agriculture in 1932 and 1933.

classes had been treated as material, to be manipulated this way and that. They had reacted by forming their own organisations and political parties in opposition to the State. The task now is, in a catch-phrase of the Nazis, to " de-proletarianise " the masses, to abolish the " masses ", to give every man responsibility and control. The situation of the peasantry was the nearest so far to this ideal, each peasant being responsible for his own farm, and organised in Chambers of Agriculture which even under the Weimar Constitution were recognised and consulted by the government. Even here, however, much is lacking, for under these most favourable circumstances acute differences often arose between small and large landowners.

This opposition to liberalistic capitalism and proletarian politics has a long tradition in Germany. It became a clearly defined revolt at the beginning of the period of industrialisation, and found its first exponent in Adam Müller. Among others of its early partisans the most important are Görres, H. von Thünen, and Friedrich List. It has remained strong in Catholic circles, nurtured especially in the Görres Society, with its own periodicals and encyclopedia. Nowadays, outside of National-Socialist groups, Othmar Spann is its chief theorist, and he has been of great influence in the popularisation of the idea of the Corporate State. It is no accident that the " Corporate State " in Austria has been introduced by the Catholic Dolfuss in co-operation with the Catholic Trade Unions.

The National-Socialists have taken much from

these Catholic theorists, especially the anti-materialistic aspect and the view that the worker must be raised to a position of personal responsibility. The Corporation is viewed as an " association for production " in which every member participates.[1] Frauendorfer, in the official publications of the National-Socialist Party, praises the idea of the Factory Councils for this very reason, because through them the worker is prevented from seeing himself merely as the " object " of the economic system; he even goes so far as to admire the Soviet system from this point of view, and demands a National-Socialist modification of it.[2] In July 1933 the Jesuit Grundbach found it necessary to warn the Nazi government that it was running entirely counter to the ideas of the Corporate State, since it seemed to be establishing corporations in the old sense, as institutions of privilege, and to be plunging the working-class ever deeper into the mire of depressed masses.

There is no very clear National-Socialist plan of the Corporative State, certainly no authoritative one. Frauendorfer gives a typical sketch of what was hoped for. The lowest units of the Corporate structure are the Regional Unions of the workers (manual), of the employees (clerks, etc.), and of the employers of a certain industry. These Unions combined form the Regional Federation, on which all are equally repre-

[1] Cf. Gustav Grundbach in the periodical *Stimmen der Zeit*, July 1933.

[2] Max Frauendorfer, *Der Ständische Gedanke im Nationalsozialismus*, 3rd edition, 1933, p. 27. Frauendorfer is now a high official of the Labour Front.

sented. Further the Regional Unions are enlarged geographically to form higher organs of the workers, employees, and employers, which are again united together to form Federations of all the three. The National Unions of workers, employees and employers are called Chambers, and each elects representatives to compose the National Economic Council. Similarly formed are the Economic Councils for Agriculture, Industry, Trade, etc. This type of organisation, says Frauendorfer, serves two main purposes. Firstly, the organs of the Corporations are executive bodies, and make it possible to carry through a vigorous policy all through the Corporation. Secondly, it " overcomes the democratic spirit " ; i.e. every man is given a sphere of labour and a proper share in the direction and control of his labour, but is prevented from busying himself with the political interests of his specific class. Any political control over the State is annulled, and as a consolation men are allowed to take a responsible part in the productive process. The " class-war " is abolished ; in place of proletarians we shall have members of a Corporation.

The whole crux of the Corporate State is then this—that particular interests are forbidden from forming political parties to serve their own ends, but are given, according to their position in the productive process, power over their own destinies. Employers, say the theorists, " Marxist ", " liberalistic " employers, have misused their powers, and will be controlled by the Corporation. The workers have been exploited, they have not been allowed to be human beings to the full, and have reacted by class-organisation and class-ideology. The class-struggle has brought " civilisation " to the brink of ruin. Class-organisations must be broken, and the worker given his full place in society. Thus the adherents of the Corporate State had continually to warn Germany against the fate of Italy. In Italy they saw no effective control over rapacious capitalism ; and at the same time the organisation of the workers was a farce. Fascist officials ruled the Trade Unions, and the workers remained without control over their Corporations. Many of the Nazi theorists conjured the Hitler government not to touch the Trade Unions as they were in 1932. They pointed out that wages and working conditions in Italy were not determined by the workers at all, but by the government. Politics, they say, the general plan for industry and trade, must be laid down by the State. But all other economic questions should lie within the competence of the Corporations—not merely wage-rates and working conditions, insurance, etc., but also judiciary powers in matters concerning the Corporations. The life-blood of the Corporation is power and self-determination. Only so can its members feel themselves a living part of the national organism, the " racial community ".

It should be emphasised that the vast amount of discussion on the subject of the Corporate State was neither homogeneous nor constructive. It never crystallised into a programme ; the Nazi leaders very decidedly rejected the idea that they were working according to any programme ; nor, of course, did it establish any separate political organisation or leadership. Its fundamental political assumption was, that the National-Socialist Party under the leadership of Hitler would effect reforms of this kind. It was, however, characteristic of the National-Socialist Party that its propaganda adapted itself to different times and different social classes. Even Alfred Rosenberg, a man who is linked up closely with big capitalist interests, could at one time suggest a land-reform directed against the big landowners. Gregor Strasser was utilised to talk specially to the working-class. Providing there is no discussion of the actual political hindrances and political methods needed, the National-Socialist Party, like Mussolini's and Mosley's Fascists, encourages vague talk of ideal reforms ; the Party must, however, retain its absolute organisatory and political control, the principle of leadership must not be assailed.

For the characteristic of all these schemes of the radical wing of the National-Socialist Party is, that there is no definition of what the State is, nor of the means by which it is to be changed. The State is considered by them to be an absolute ; their vituperation they turn merely against certain elements within the state. Their theories are expediential, superficial, because they aim not at reorganising society, but at cutting back certain excrescences of society, of capitalism. And in spite of their apotheosis of "politics", they have no theory of revolt, of the means of winning power. There is a sharp distinction between works on the Storm Troops—like those of Killinger or Röhm, which hold up to admiration the spirit of organised ruffianliness—and works on the aims of National-Socialism. These radicals do not in any way suggest how their ideas are to be put into practice, how they are going to overcome the powers that be. But ideas do not conquer the world. It was not ideas that gave the Storm Troops the freedom of the streets, that clothed them in new uniforms, that put Hitler into the Chancellorship.

And finally, these theoreticians of the Corporate State do not discuss the leadership of their ideal society. When workers and employers are represented equally in one Council, when different branches of industry are hammering out a unified policy, who is to decide when differences arise? The Catholic Parties had advocated such an organisation partly because under such circumstances the Church itself would have a more decisive role than at present. The Nazis would no doubt answer, the National-Socialist Party would have this role of leader or mediator. But what is the National-Socialist Party? What, in the Corporate State, would be the qualifications of membership? It is impossible to deduce this by abstract reason. It should stand for the "welfare of the whole nation"; but this welfare is differently understood by different groups of interest. And however much these differences can be reconciled amongst the leaders of industry, they can never be eliminated as between workers and employers. Since there is the alternative of a socialist society, of a society where the capitalist class is abolished—and the existence and strength of Soviet Russia cannot be hidden—the demands of the workers cannot be finally reconciled with those of their employers. The leadership of the State, therefore, in the hands of the National-Socialist Party, must declare itself for the one dominant group of interest of the capitalists, and against the interests of the workers. This fundamental problem is ignored by the writers on the Corporate State; yet it is round this fact that the whole policy of the National-Socialist State revolves.

CHAPTER VIII

HITLER TAKES OVER POWER

HITLER became Chancellor on January 30, at the head of a government of national concentration in which the old ultra-conservative Party, the Nationalists, held a reassuring majority. He had, however, control over the Ministry of the Interior and the Prussian police, and had further the prospect of *Reichstag* elections on March 5, which he had made a condition of his participation in the government. He set to work to consolidate his position, and to make sure that the elections would bring the victorious smashing-through of the National-Socialist Party.

Almost the first act of the new Minister of the Interior, Frick, was a decree forbidding all meetings and demonstrations where any attack—even only verbal—was made on the new government. The police were given extraordinary powers to deal with such meetings. The Opposition Press was confiscated and banned. Socialist and Communist papers were to all intents and purposes prohibited ; incitement to strike was made a reason for confiscation. Frick was given especial powers for dealing with provincial authorities who should show themselves loath to carry out these stringent orders. On February 21 there followed an uncompromising prohibition of Communist demonstrations and open-air meetings in Saxony.

At the same time Göring, now in command of the Prussian police, began the activity which has made him famous as a man of action. He finished the administrative work begun by Von Papen as Commissar for Prussia, rooting out the last relics of " unreliable " elements in the police force. All men suspected of socialist or communist sympathies were summarily dismissed, and his own men, Storm Troopers, were put in their places.[1] On February 17 he was secure enough to issue the first of his many half-raving, blood-drunken decrees—the police is to support the S.A. and the S.S. absolutely ; against communistic " acts of terror " extreme methods are to be adopted—" Police officials who make use of their guns in the execution of their duty will be covered by my personal authority, whatever the result of their actions ; whoever, on the other hand, fails out of false considerations must expect punishment." This is the voice of the man who, in the Court of Law at Leipzig, threatened open vengeance on the accused Dimitröff. Five days later Göring took the step which assured the success of the Hitler Party. He proclaimed that the police force was not strong enough in numbers to cope with the situation. An auxiliary police force was created, with a special uniform, provided with batons and revolvers. Fifty per cent of the Auxiliary Police were recruited from

[1] In Göring's own words : " Out of 32 police chiefs I removed 22. Hundreds of inspectors and thousands of police sergeants followed in the course of the next month. New men were brought in, and in every case these men came from the great reservoir of the Storm Troops and Guards (S.A. and S.S.)." Göring *Germany Reborn*, p. 121.

the S.A., 30 per cent from the S.S., and 20 per cent from the nationalist defence corps, the Steel Helmets. The whole number recruited in Prussia is estimated at 50,000.

The National-Socialists went on to assure themselves of the support of the peasants. On February 14 the peasants were protected from compulsory bankruptcy. Three days later tariffs were increased all round in order to make the home market secure. On February 22 credits of 100 million marks were granted to stimulate repairs, additions, etc. to farm buildings —a measure calculated to win over the Unemployed to the side of the Nazis. Further steps were taken for the peasants in the months that followed. Tenant-farmers were given the same protection from bankruptcy as peasants. A more concrete step was Hugenberg's last official Act before he was dismissed from his post as Minister for Agriculture. The high-sounding title of this Act is the "Law for the Liquidation of Agricultural Debts". Interest-rates were compulsorily lowered to 4½ per cent. It was characteristic of Nazi politics that Hugenberg's Nazi rivals vehemently opposed this "usury", and called for a maximum rate of 2 per cent. Darré, Hugenberg's successor, and now Minister for Agriculture, led this radical demand—though when he came into office he found it best to leave matters as they were. These concessions to the peasantry, together with the radical talk of the Nazis, won the peasants over to the Nazi cause for the time being. It is true that there was a widespread hope and belief that the great estates would be broken up and given to the smaller peasantry. But this demand was fended off with promises to the poor and exhortations to the rich. Here and there a few acres of inferior land were voluntarily put at the disposal of the government by the big landowners.

The technical weapons of Nazi oppression, the armed Storm Troopers and the centralised control of the administration, were now forged. Their rear was guarded through the temporary goodwill of the masses of the agricultural population. There remained the other side, the incitement of the masses, the propaganda which was to sweep wavering public opinion into the Nazi camp. But propaganda was the Nazis' strong point. Their fertility and ingenuity in stimulating enthusiasm was boundless. With the Press and Radio practically completely in their hands they stopped at nothing. While Hitler was reassuring foreign and home opinion of the constitutional and pacific intentions of his party, the onslaught on the Opposition was prepared and begun; and it is as well to bear in mind this double-tonguedness of the Nazis when any official pronouncement is made.

The Suppression of the Communists

While other political organisations were tolerated, while some working-class leaders, Trade Unionists (for instance Leipart, the President of the Socialist General Confederation of Trade Unions) were protesting their willingness to co-operate in a Nazi State, the Nazis directed the spearhead of their attack against the Communists. It was a condition of their success that the working-class should be split.

The Socialist and Trade Union leaders had not responded to the Communist call for a general strike at the time of Papen's *coup d'état* in Prussia, and again on Hitler's accession to power. Hitler skilfully exploited this disunity to isolate the Communists and crush them while the Social-Democrats remained neutral.

By the end of February the Communist Party had scarcely any Press or right of association. It was already carrying on its work under conditions of illegality. But the Nazis aimed at violent eradication, and needed a sensation in order to inflame passions. On February 24 the police of Göring, following a time-honoured practice, raided the Communist headquarters in Berlin—the Karl Liebknecht house. Many raids had been carried out in the preceding three years, all with no result. By 1933 the Communist leadership had left the Karl Liebknecht house, and certainly there was nothing of political importance left there. However, the report of the official Nazi press agency contained hair-raising accounts of the discoveries in the " subterranean cellars ". Three days later Göring supplemented the report with the announcement that extensive plans for a Communist terror had been discovered, plans for poisoning wells, burning buildings, murder. He promised further details for the future; they have alas not been forthcoming. The whole trick was a little stale and did not produce the desired effect. And so the People was granted a real thrill—the burning of the *Reichstag*.

The story of the *Reichstag* fire has often been told,

especially in connexion with the trial of the accused. On the evening of February 27 the *Reichstag* was found in flames. Marinus van der Lubbe, a Dutch youth who had been expelled from the Dutch Communist Party some years previously, was found on the premises. He confessed the authorship of the fire, which he said he had carried out with fire-lighters. He had made attempts on other public buildings, which had failed. Within a few minutes of the discovery of the fire, Hitler, Göring and other Nazi leaders were on the spot. The "Leader" exclaimed that the Communists were responsible for the outrage. An official Press report announced, contrary to the facts, that Van der Lubbe had a membership card of the Communist Party in his possession. This was all that was necessary. The prejudices of the middle-class Parties against violent repression were removed. Göring and the armed Storm Troops were put in command of Germany, and the Terror began.

There is no space here to enter into the pros and cons concerning the origin of the fire. Certain it is that the Communist Party has always turned its face resolutely against acts of terrorism and individual terrorists. The trial, in which four Communists were arraigned alongside Van der Lubbe, showed no connexion between the Communist Party and the fire. Certain it is that the fire turned exclusively to the advantage of the Nazis, whose whole terroristic organisation was prepared for this moment. The responsibility of the Nazis has never been officially investigated. Men who according to widespread knowledge were in touch with evidence of Nazi guilt were killed—the clairvoyant Hanussen, the confidant of Count Helldorf, the chief of the Berlin Storm Troops ; the Nationalist Dr. Oberfohren, author of a memorandum on the fire ; the National-Socialist, Dr. Bell, the friend of Röhm and other leaders, who got clear of Germany only to be murdered in an Austrian village by a raid from the German frontier. On June 30, 1934, those Nazi leaders publicly rumoured to be connected with the Fire, Heines, Ernst, etc., were killed on Hitler's orders. Van der Lubbe himself, half out of his wits, perhaps doped, answered only one question clearly in the trial—that he had spent some time " with the Nazis ". The trial in Leipzig had the effect of stirring up in foreign nations a deep anger and scorn of Hitlerism. And it provided the setting for an heroic personality to impress himself on the imagination of the world, Dimitroff, the Bulgarian Communist leader. Poor Van der Lubbe paid for the fire with his head.[1]

But whatever the authorship of the fire and the outcome of the trial the fire did its work. All Germany was ablaze. That righteous indignation which Hitlerism needed filled the floodgates of the Nazi Party. On the 28th of February Hitler issued a decree " for the protection of State and People ". All the liberties of the Weimar Republic were suspended, never to return. All treasonable acts were declared punishable by death or imprisonment—and treasonable was to be construed, opposed to the

[1] For the *Reichstag* fire, read, among innumerable books and pamphlets, the two *Brown Books of the Hitler Terror*, published by Gollancz, and Douglas Reed, *The Reichstag Trial*.

government. The government was given power over all provincial bodies. But differently from in other cases when a State of Emergency had been declared, the police, not the army, was given full control. And the police meant Göring and Röhm, the Storm Troops. Immediately, all over the country, all Communist *Reichstag* deputies and leaders to be found were taken into " protective custody ". Local leaders suffered especially, being well known to the Storm Troopers. The Communist Press was entirely banned and became illegal from this time on. Within two weeks the whole working-class Press was banned too. What happened in protective custody is a terrible story. The victims were usually taken first to the " Brown Houses ", the Nazi headquarters, and there ill-treated ; when the number of prisoners became too large to be held in the Brown Houses, the Concentration Camps were everywhere organised. Sickening horrors took place. Murders and suicides followed on beatings, rape, and torture. In Prussia alone, within 48 hours of the Fire, over 4,000 persons were put into protective custody. The rapidity of action, the similarity of procedure all over Germany indicated that everything was planned in advance and directed from above. On March 21 the death-penalty was imposed for all sorts of political crimes, and special courts were instituted to deal with the Opposition.

In this panic the *Reichstag* Elections of March 5 were held. The Left opposition Parties were without a Press and under a terror. The Nazis were in possession of the most effective means of propaganda, the

Press and the Radio, and had the only effective election machine. Yet, in spite of this, they did not gain an absolute majority. The figures were :

National-Socialists . . .	288 seats
Social-Democrats . . .	120 ,,
Communists	81 ,,
Centre	73 ,,
German Nationalists . . .	52 ,,

The National-Socialists were still, apparently, dependent on their allies the Nationalists for a majority. But the Nazi methods were simple. The Communists were either in prison or virtually outlawed. Thus they had their majority. And even without a majority, the pressure from beneath, the Terror of the Storm Troopers, was sufficient to bend other Parties to their wishes.

From the moment of Hitler's accession to power the *Reichstag*, as the symbol of democracy and as an executive body, ceases to have any power. Hitler could afford to use conciliatory phrases. The real power was in the hands of the Nazi organisation—and the rapidity with which the transformation of Germany was carried out bears witness to the power of this organisation in the March and April days of 1933. On March 8 the Nazis proceeded to take all power in the provinces into their hands. On this day Frick, as Minister of the Interior, nominated police commissars for Baden, Würtemberg, Saxony, and Schaumberg-Lippe. All were of course Nazi leaders. In Baden the S.A. leader Wagner forced the elected government to capitulate and established his supreme authority, under Frick. All the ministries were filled with Nazis. In Hamburg the Nazi District Leader forced the Senate to resign, and a Nazi was elected burgomaster. The most spectacular success was scored in Bavaria, where traditional separatism promised trouble for the centralising aims of the Nazis. The Catholic government under Held made mock-heroic gestures of defiance. Frick sent General von Epp, the man who had liberated Munich in 1919 from the Communists, to take over the police. Röhm was sent in his support. The Storm Troops poured into the streets in dense masses. Held had principles but no power, and his government faded out. On March 12 Hitler arrived at his beloved Munich to announce that the great National Revolution was effected. The control of the provincial police and administration marks the first stage of the National-Socialist revolution, the frame-work within which its further plans were to be fashioned.

Thus the setting was given for the opening of the new *Reichstag*. It was initiated with a solemn ceremony at the church in Potsdam, when Prussia's military past was invoked, and all the paraphernalia of national symbols, not excluding Hindenburg, were exploited to the full. In its first business-session the *Reichstag* passed the Enabling Act, renouncing all control over Hitler's government for a space of four years. Henceforth the *Reichstag* was called together only as a propagandist step, to listen to the pronouncements of Hitler and to signify its consent. From this *Reichstag* the Communist Party was of course absent. Only the Social-Democrats refused to join in the vote of confidence in Hitler. The Catholic Centre gave him its allegiance, trusting in his promise that the rights of the Church would be respected and that all Parties would be consulted by the government. Hitler promised further a " quiet German development and rapprochement which would grow in the future ". The Catholics were only too eager to listen to these promises—events since then have shown how far they have been kept. During the *Reichstag* session armed Storm Troopers filled the hall and passages of the building (the Kroll opera house). Such was the formal end of the Weimar Republic.

The National-Socialist élan had been launched by the *Reichstag* fire, and borne along by the terror against Communists and other radical elements. Once the extermination of the Communist organisations was entered upon, there was no calling a halt. The complete centralisation of authority in the hands of the National-Socialist party was the result of the determination to eradicate Communism. The old bourgeois Parties were ready to react favourably to the mass-suggestion of the Nazi propagandists—now practically in complete charge of the means of publicity—and could do nothing but give the Storm Troops their head. But Hitler was as thorough as he was prepared. The Terror was responsible for smashing individual and local resistance to the new regime. Hitler foresaw the time when local Nazi initiative would have to be curbed, and quickly laid the foundation for a centralised administration which would dominate permanently all disaffected elements, even, if necessary, the S.A. itself. Eight days after the Enabling Act the first of the " Co-ordination " (*Gleichschaltung*) laws was passed, a series of laws which took away the independence of all bodies which were not National-Socialist, whether political, social, industrial, religious, educational, professional or recreational.

This first Co-ordination law follows the usual plan of Hitler's tactics—covering over its robbery of fundamental rights with cajolery and fair promises. It was decreed that all Provincial Assemblies (representing the German States, provinces, districts, municipalities, etc.) were to be dissolved, and formed anew on the basis of the number of votes cast in the *Reichstag* election of March 5—the Communist vote to be disregarded. Thus the National-Socialists were assured of a majority in practically all these bodies, as a result of the " ramp " vote of March 5. It was expressly affirmed that the " institution of these legislative bodies itself was not to be assailed ". But this was a tactical step. The existence of any democratic institutions is a danger for a Hitlerite dictatorship. On April 7 a further " Co-ordination " law was decreed, supplementing or rather superseding the former. Lieutenants (*Statthalter*) were appointed by Hitler as supreme rulers of the various States, responsible directly to Hitler, and instruments of the political line of the Nazi Party. They were given power to nominate the presidents of the Provincial Assemblies, to dissolve the Assemblies when they thought fit, to dismiss officials. Later their powers were extended so that they had the sole right of initiating laws in the Assemblies—an exception being made for Prussia, where Hitler, as Lieutenant, delegated his powers to Göring as Minister-President of Prussia. Later still, on January 30, 1934, the Provincial Assemblies were finally dissolved, and the Lieutenants were left as sole, dictatorial governors of the provinces.[1] Even in Prussia, after a long struggle for hegemony, Göring had to resign his office of Minister of the Interior, in favour of the *Reich* Minister of the Interior, Frick, retaining only the Prussian police. So efficiently did the Nazis utilise the upheaval that all positions of power were captured, from which their tentacles spread into the last lairs of self-government.

The Persecution of the Jews

The Terror which had opened in February had been a part of a consistent and thorough attack on the Communists and militant working-class elements. Its theoretical justification was the cause of national unity. But this same principle of unity turned the Terror against the Jews—and it was this aspect which loomed most prominently in the eyes of world-opinion and which was mainly responsible for earning the Hitlerite regime its present unenviable reputation for barbarism. Even in Germany, and in circles favourable to Hitler, the Anti-Semitism

[1] The Lieutenants were given the salary of a Minister of the *Reich*, plus all expenses incurred in the execution of their duties, plus a house (or, in lieu of a house, 3,600 marks annually).

of the Nazis had not been taken seriously. Hitler himself had been more and more moderate with respect to the Jews as he approached power. German Jews, too, did not as a rule expect any violent attack—a great number of the well-to-do Jews used to vote for the German Nationalist Party, which they knew was flirting with Hitler all through 1932. In the first two months of the Hitler government there was no legislation against the Jews. But the nationalism of the Nazis was largely based on racialism. Numberless cases of petty persecution occurred in Germany all through the period of the Weimar Republic, and many outrages had taken place in 1932, cases of individual terror and open riot against Jewish shops. In pamphlets and periodicals the incitement to hate and destroy the Jews never stopped—as in the Nürnberg paper, *Der Stürmer*, of the Hitlerite leader Streicher, or such pamphlets as *Jews Look at You* with its distorted facts and pictures. And so, when the S.A. was armed and the Terror let loose, the Jews suffered as severely—as far as individuals were concerned—as the Communists. Mishandled in their homes and on the streets, the helpless and unprepared Jews were subject to horrible and ignominious torture in the Concentration camps.

In its first stages the Terror against the Jews bore a purely racial character. It was directed indiscriminately against all classes of Jews, a true pogrom. Radical Jews, particularly publicists, were treated worst, perhaps, and special attacks were made on the Big Stores which were owned by Jews. But, on the surface at any rate, the persecution did not bear any clear trace of a social origin. It has been described how, in the theory of the National-Socialist party, the polemic against finance-capital and capitalism in general was more or less identical with an attack on Jewish capital and property.[1] In this way the socialist edge was taken off the sword of Nazi propaganda. Now, in the first months of power, the Nazi government was unwilling to make a controlled drive even on the banking and usurious Jews, for fear of rousing too vigorously anti-capitalist feelings. The persecution of the Jews was kept, as far as possible, as a racial and personal Terror instead of a social one. The passions which it let loose were not social passions, but personal passions of the basest kind. They took varied forms ; men were maimed and tortured, socially and morally pilloried, held up to public ridicule in the cruellest way. But, though much of Hitler's riff-raff were satisfied with this outlet of their passions, and though many others were carried away by the opinions current in ruling circles, many demanded that the attack on the Jews should fulfil its original intention—i.e. should be, in some sort, an onslaught against finance-capital and Big Business. Hitler, it seems, would have been glad for the whole Jewish terror to have exhausted itself naturally, and did not wish to take steps to organise it or to meddle with it. But pressure from the S.A. was brought to bear—and from an S.A. which was not, as to-day, disciplined and controlled, but which was in the full tide of its armed " revolutionary " advance. Goebbels made himself the

[1] See Chapter V, pp. 68–70, 79–80.

spokesman of the restive elements. He persuaded Hitler to sanction an organised boycott of Jewish shops for April 1. It was the first concession to the "revolutionary" lower middle-class, which was to carry through this economic, social step against the Big Stores, which were mainly in the hands of Jews. So, on April 1, all Jewish shops throughout Germany were labelled prominently, armed Storm Troopers stood outside the doors to "warn" the people from entering. The boycott, which was prolonged till April 5, was proclaimed as a disciplined and dignified protest against the Jews.

But even in this matter the government were anxious to avoid the socialist flavour of the action. Julius Streicher, the fanatical leader of the Nürnberg Nazis, who had been put in charge of the whole boycott operation, wished to see it as a direct offensive against the Jews. The government, however, justified it to Germans and to the world as an answer to the stories of Anti-Semitic atrocities which were radiating from Germany into foreign countries. To combat these stories a special Ministry for Propaganda and Enlightenment had been established on March 13, with Goebbels at its head, having powers to trespass on the business of all other departments of State. Draconic measures had been passed against the "bearers of atrocity-lies", against all private and public complaints against the Terror. The grand boycott action was excused by Hitler as a protest against these stories.

The effects of the Jewish persecution abroad were far-reaching. Private and concerted boycotts of

German goods were undertaken, which have contributed to the closing of the foreign market to Germany in certain types of goods. This boycott was strongest in the United States of America, where Jewish commercial interests are strong. For a time, and even now, this boycott is, however, resisted by Jewish merchants in Germany. Jewish importance in Germany's economic life is greatest in the export trade. For long Jewish export businesses were not touched by the Anti-Semitic persecution, and these merchants saw that the boycott of German goods would, and did, hurt them. Concerted Jewish action has therefore mainly taken the form of philanthropic relief rather than economic action. In England incriminations against this half-hearted and diplomatic policy have resulted, with bitter quarrels in the ranks of the Jews themselves.

But the political results of the Hitlerite action against the Jews have been more remarkable. Even easy-going citizens of the capitalist countries, who were inclined to welcome Hitler's oppression of the Communists, were horrified by the outbreak of the Jewish pogrom. Their view was summed up by Sir Austen Chamberlain in an outspoken speech in the House of Commons. He described the spirit of the pogrom as that of the worst Prussian imperialism, and pointed out that these same principles would lead to the justification of the extirpation of the Poles or of any other race. The pro-France policy of Sir Austen Chamberlain received thus its justification. The old hatred of Prussianism, which during the period of the Republic had received little credence or support in more progressive circles, proudly vindicated itself. Anti-Semitism, whose socialistic aspect was throttled by the Nazi leaders, served only national ends, and revealed more clearly than other actions the militaristic aims of National-Socialism.

The pogrom against the person of the Jews had, however, a harmful effect in other ways. Trade particularly suffered ; and the Germans did not gain anything concrete. In April the Nazi government began an Anti-Semitic policy which is still now, in 1934, in full blast, and which has caused greater satisfaction among some of the Nazi supporters. This programme can be summed up as the policy of replacing Jews who are not indispensable to the State with " Aryans ". There is no change of system, of social policy, Jewish individuals are simply thrown out and Non-Jews put in their place. It is possible that this principle has a great place in the whole history of National-Socialism. Thyssen, the powerful industrialist, of the German Steel Trust, *in extremis* during 1932, had seen that a necessary condition of his own rehabilitation was the elimination of his rival in the Steel Trust Otto Wolff. Anti-Semitism was a useful weapon in the struggle between the two groups, for Wolff was closely associated with Catholic-Jewish business circles. Under Hitler Thyssen and Vögler, his lieutenant, have attained to high administrative posts, while the rival group has been subordinated to them. Wolff's associate, the Jew Wassermann, was forced to resign from his post as Managing-Director of the *Deutsche Bank*, and from the Board of the *Reichsbank*. His Jewish partners, Othmar Strauss and Silverberg, were thrust into obscurity.

In April this principle of making places free by the removal of Jews was applied to the whole of the administration of Germany. By a series of laws for the "restoration" of the official classes, Jews were dismissed from all State-posts. Officials of the administration, lawyers and doctors, professors, teachers in universities, technical colleges, and schools, scientific workers were all combed out. Certain qualifications were made, especially in the case of former front-soldiers, but these qualifications have been frequently ignored. Further, in a law of April 25, concerning overcrowding in German universities and schools, the number of Jewish pupils was restricted to a percentage corresponding to the proportion of Jews in the district concerned—although, of course, the closing of the professions to the Jews makes academic education of dubious value to them. To have one Jewish grandparent stamps one as Non-Aryan.

With the passage of these laws began the great Jewish exodus from Germany. Thousands of Jews, left without the means of making a livelihood, fled abroad and threw themselves on the mercy of foreigners. Many, hopeless, committed suicide. In May 1934 the Academic Assistance Council published a report with the names of 1,202 university teachers and research-workers who had been displaced by these decrees. Of these 389 had found places abroad, most of them being temporary posts for one year. But this list does not include the thousands of lawyers, doctors, minor officials, etc., who are suffering.[1]

The indignation at the persecution of the Jews, which resulted in protests from all over the world, has begun to die down. To some extent it is believed that the persecution has grown less. Certainly methods of open terror are less ; there is no longer an open boycott. But the position of the Jews in Germany is rapidly deteriorating. In April 1933 it was declared that Jewish business men would be free of injury—" If the factory-stacks smoke, we shall not ask whether the owner has a Non-Aryan grandparent ". But in 1934 Mortgage Markets were established in Hamburg and Cologne from which Jews were excluded. Jewish business managers are being dismissed. According to a decision of Dr. Ley, the leader of the German Labour Front, Jewish owners of factories may not assume the position of " Leader " of the factory, as this contends with the principle of the National-Socialist community. Jews are not allowed to be apprenticed to farmers. On April 19 it was announced that Prussian schools need not observe the strict proportion between Aryans and Non-Aryans, but should give every preference to the former. The special Jewish schools were forbidden to enter new children this year. These are all official measures which show the general policy of the Hitler government towards the Jews.

[1] From April 7, 1933, to April 1, 1934, the number of Non-Aryan lawyers fell by 38·84 per cent., the number of Non-Aryan notaries by 56·79 per cent. The *Frankfurter Zeitung* reckoned that about 2,000 doctors have lost their practices, most of them being Jews.

The practical, day-to-day expression of this policy is the interminable series of acts of petty and malicious torture which provide titbits for the German newspapers. Such, for instance, is the pillorying of Aryan girls who are seen to keep the company of Jews. The chief cesspool from which this filth filters all over Germany—with the tacit approval of Hitler—is the periodical *Der Stürmer*, the editor of which is Julius Streicher. A few days before this man formally took office as Chief Political Officer in the government of Lower Franconia, in May 1934, his most worthy effort was published—a description of the "ritual-murders" of the Jews, with descriptions and illustrations from all the most scurrilous Anti-Semitic publications of modern times, and, as "scientific" proof, reproductions of Anti-Semitic agitation of the Middle Ages. It is a vicious incitement to a pogrom. Its toleration in a country where even printing errors may bring suspension of a paper, is sign of the complicity of the leaders of the Nazi movement. There is no doubt that the persecution of the Jews in Germany is continuing, is brooding out further attacks, will stop at nothing if it serves the purpose of the Nazis.

It is of the utmost importance to make account to oneself of the real significance of the Jewish persecution in Germany. In some circles, often among Jews themselves, it is looked on as proof of moral viciousness in the German race—in this sense it is used by certain politicians to re-kindle the old hatred of barbarian Prussianism. In other circles, notably Left political circles, it is sometimes looked on as a mere incident in the general plan of Hitlerism, the crushing of the working-class. But it is a fundamental part of the reactionary framework of National-Socialism. The elder Liebknecht called Anti-Semitism the " fools' socialism ". The traditional Anti-Semitism of the western world has been associated with the hatred of Jews as bankers and traders. In the German peasants' wars of the fifteenth and sixteenth centuries Jewish usurers were threatened together with princes and landowners. Hitler's Anti-Semitism has always coupled personal prejudice for the Jews with loathing for them as bankers, publicists, lawyers, etc. Now it is very significant that, while the Jews were essential to Germany, during the nineteenth century, because of their experience and connexions in trade and banking, in science and economics, Anti-Semitism lurked harmless. Since the War they have become much less important in Germany. As bankers they could be replaced by other Aryan banking houses, in the professions they prevented Aryans from rising. Some loss was incurred by eliminating them from activity, but there are not many Einsteins, and the loss could be borne. In Italy Anti-Semitism is not an official policy, since the stage of economic development is nearer to that of nineteenth-century Germany.

The Jewish persecution of 1933 and 1934 arose as the direct result of the need for radical reform and the impotence of the Jews to make themselves essential to the State. The radical attack in the National-Socialist theory on banks, stock-exchange, and big industry was made more harmless by turning it into an attack on *Jewish* bankers, brokers, and merchants.

The final step transformed this attack again into an attack on the Jewish race itself, and especially on radical, " intellectual " Jews, who supported parties of the Left. This naturally has not provided the hoped-for satisfaction for the masses who hoped for some sort of social change. Individuals, especially of the professional classes, have gained better jobs. These are welded closer to the National-Socialist State. The masses are given the satisfaction of racial passion and individual terror. As long as the general economic position in Germany does not improve, as long as there is no social reform, the Nazi leaders will be bound to foment racial passion against the Jews as an outlet for the discontent of their followers. This is Streicher's function at the moment, to prepare the masses. The possibility of a pogrom in the Czarist fashion lies in the sphere of practical politics.

The Trade Unions

There was no doubt in the minds of the Nazi leaders as to where the real enemy lay. They utilised the split in the ranks of the working-class to suppress the Communist organisations. After cleansing all the administrative apparatus and centralising control they made their onslaught on the Trade Unions and the Social-Democratic Party—and so well had they prepared their attack that the fortress fell almost without a struggle, another Jericho.

The Trade Unions had been the pride of the Social-Democratic Party. The " Free " Trade Unions, organised together in the United Trade Unions (A.D.G.B.), had formed the basis of the Socialist movement. They were recognised by the State, exercised many and responsible constitutional functions, and were highly disciplined. Even during the worst period of the crisis the mass of the organised union-men held fast to the Socialist Party, and continued to vote for it. But during 1932 evidences of weakness and wavering in allegiance were to be remarked, and a growing dissension between the leaders and the rank and file. In the strikes at the end of 1932 Social-Democratic influence was being overwhelmed by Communist. Much dissatisfaction was expressed by the rank and file with the policy of compromise between Trade-Union leaders and the governments of Brüning and Papen. The number of paying members dwindled—some going to the Communists, some disheartened leaving affairs to settle themselves, few however joining up with the Nazis.

Much of the propaganda of Gregor Strasser was directed towards winning over the Trade Unions. In May 1932 he met leaders of the Unions. Later in the year, during his negotiations with the Chancellor Schleicher, the question of forming a *bloc* with the Trade Unions was played with. Strasser's radicalism made this seem a possibility. Hans Zehrer, the editor of *Die Tat*, who was entrusted by Schleicher with important publicist responsibility, urged now and later the necessity of incorporating the Trade Unions, as they were, in the leadership of the State. These schemes were based on the correct appreciation of the fact that the Trade Unions were driving more and more to a " national " policy—Leipart in October confessed his faith in the " National Idea ", and published a conciliatory article in Otto Strasser's paper *Schwarze Front*—and were anxious to preserve their organisation at any cost. But they failed, both because of the lack of support for Schleicher's regime, and because of the growing dissensions in the Trade Unions themselves.

When Hitler came to power the United Trade Unions reconciled themselves with the concrete facts, and tried to preserve their own existence. Leipart, their president, stated that they would be an organised but controlled Opposition. He, with other leaders, sought to ingratiate the movement in Hitler's favour by stating that the Unions had nothing to say to the political developments of the time. On March 21 Leipart sent a letter to Hitler, claiming for the Unions only the right of participation in social and economic matters touching the workers. On April 1 the organ of the Metal Workers' Union, the largest German Trade Union, announced that it would solidly and loyally work together with Hitler's movement to eliminate the economic distress of the country. With this as their policy the Trade Unions stood quietly by while the Communist Party was being annihilated—looking on with a certain amount of satisfaction at the discomfiture of their old foes. On the 7th of April, the day when local and provincial governments were made subject to Hitler's Lieutenants, Leipart proclaimed that the Trade Unions "recognised the great aims of the government", and claimed recognition for the Trade Unions from Hitler. He stated that they should be entrusted with the legal functions of representing labour in the Labour Courts, of organising accident and health insurance, etc. But all this willingness to conform to the National-Socialist State helped the Trade Unions little. Hitler waited until other enemies were weakened, until the administration was prepared, and then levelled his blow. Leipart was asked to resign. While he hesitated the blow fell.

The Nazis prepared their attack cleverly. The first step was to secure the factories as far as possible, so as to obviate the possibility of a general strike. Two methods were open to the Nazi government. One was Hugenberg's plan, the organisation of "yellow" Trade Unions, Company Unions, associations led by the employers with the frank intention of breaking strikes. The other method was the organisation, within the factories, of National-Socialist cells on a general political basis, which emphasised the more radical side of the general Nazi propaganda. This latter method prevailed, and was the right one. The company unions excited the greatest anger in the ranks of the members of the Free Trade Unions, being frankly reactionary. But the Nazi cells also attacked these company unions, breaking up their meetings during February and March with energy, even ferocity. The Nazis preached control of employers as well as employed, a control which was to come from the Nazi Party. They were the only section of workers who could be openly active in this period, owing to the Terror, and thus gained a reputation for militancy and power which won them the tolerance if not allegiance of many former opponents. Certainly they seemed no worse, at this time, than the Social-Democratic Unions, now lifeless, capitulating, discredited.

On April 4 a law was passed providing that any worker suspected of treasonable (i.e. Communist) leanings could be dismissed without power of appeal. Further, the provincial authorities were empowered to dismiss from the factory-councils any worker who had undertaken activity " inimical to the economic system ", i.e. who had opposed the factory management, advocated strikes, etc. They were given the right to nominate the dismissed men's successors themselves, to replace them, that is, with supporters of the National-Socialist Party. In this way the opposition in the factories was removed before the general attack on the workers' organisations was opened, and the way was prepared for the final step.

Then came the typical masterstroke of Nazi tactics. May 1, Labour Day, was decreed to be a " National Holiday of Labour ". The leaders of the Trade Unions, slipping further and further down the path of compromise, called on their members to co-operate in the celebrations of the day. Their reasons were no doubt varied. Some, certainly, were mainly anxious to preserve their jobs and skins. Others thought to salvage something of the old privileges of the workers. Others again sympathised with Hitlerism, believing that the particular interests of the workers should be subordinated to those of the State.[1] Others were deluded—self-deluded—by

[1] An example is August Winnig, author of *Vom Proletariat zum Arbeitertum*, formerly a high official of Socialist Prussia, now an ardent Nazi.

Hitler's demagogy. The last issue of the *Gewerkschaftszeitung* (April 29, 1933), the organ of the Trade Unions, bears tragic witness to this. In one of the main articles the writer demands a "firm plan of nationalisation of industry" and confidently expects from Hitler the nationalisation of the banks, the key-industries, power-stations, etc. The State will take over the monopoly of foreign trade, and planned economy will replace competitive capitalism. This article, written for May 1, is an instance either of criminal gullibility, or of treacherous deceit. Under this sign the union-men marched on the Day of National Labour.

May Day was a roaring success. Masses of workers marched. The factories were closed, all the men were summoned to take part in the demonstrations. In Berlin nearly a million assembled on the *Tempelhofer Feld* to hear Hitler speak. By a special decree, renewed in 1934, men taking part in the celebrations were paid as if they were at work. More than persuasion was used. So Hitler assured himself of a good audience, which listened to a speech of the kind now common—little concrete promises apart from the announcement of the building of National Motor Roads, no question of an attack on capitalism, but much concerning honour and respect to the workman and to manual labour.

Not all the Nazis were on the streets on Labour Day. Behind the scenes plans were being laid for the real action, to which the celebrations were a dazzling façade. On the next day, May 2, contingents of Storm Troopers drove up to all Trade Union Houses all over the country. They overpowered the occupants wherever resistance was offered, and occupied the Houses. At the same time Leipart and other leaders were imprisoned and ill-treated. Whether taken by surprise or no, the Trade Unions offered no organised resistance. In some places the *Reichsbanner*, the fighting organisation of the Social-Democratic Party, made a show of fight. But no attempt was made to call a strike in their support, everywhere the members of the Unions remained quietly at work while their headquarters were being occupied. The same day Dr. Ley, who henceforth was in charge of the whole workers' organisations of Germany, could proclaim that the Trade Unions were conquered. He promised the inviolability of the institutions of the working-class, but of course all these, whether for sport, education, nature-study, or social defence, soon followed the Trade Unions and became National-Socialist property.

The Trade Unions were not simply dissolved. For the time being Nazi leaders were put into leading positions. Lower functionaries remained—were even forced to remain—in positions such as treasurers of branches, etc. The subscriptions were still collected. But instead of being institutions for protecting the workers against the employers, they became mere insurance societies. No meetings of branches were allowed, no discussions. Most of their constitutional powers passed into the hands of State (Nazi) functionaries. They were organised together, with all other workers' organisations into the German Labour Front, which is essentially an educative organisation. Its prime object, under the leadership of Dr. Ley, is to educate the workers into National-Socialist ways of thinking. It undertakes the organisation of technical classes. Employers' organisations are also included in the Labour Front. An excellent example of its educative methods is seen in Dr. Ley's speeches. They are full of man-to-man heartiness. They promise nothing concrete. At the same time they are full of expletives against the employers who are still " marxist ", advocating their sterilisation, for instance (speech of April 20, 1934, in Berlin). It is practically obligatory for workers to belong to the Labour Front. The funds are exceptionally useful to the Nazi Party. Since the Trade Unions were occupied there has been no balance-sheet published of the funds subscribed, the members do not know where the money goes. But if any man is not a member he runs the risk of being considered a treasonable subject and of losing his job. So Dr. Ley can boast of the increase in membership in his Labour Front.

The National-Socialist method of dealing with the Trade Unions is well described in an account published in the *Völkischer Beobachter* for September 17, 1933. The writer, the District Leader of the Factory Workers' Union (*Verband der Fabrikarbeiter*), formerly one of the smaller Free Trade Unions, describes how the chief task was to get rid of the " Red and Black labour-fakirs " who were filling their bellies at the expense of the workers. " With pride we can state that by August all former Marxist and Christian (in the sense of Catholic unions) Union secretaries were dismissed, and there are now in their place champions of Adolf Hitler." The result has been an increase of membership.

The culminating blow at the workers' institutions came with the establishment of governmental officials to regulate all differences between men and masters. Here the Trade-Unions had been most active. But on May 18 the old Conciliation machinery was abolished, and on May 20 Labour Trustees (*Treuhänder der Arbeit*) were nominated by the government. They were to represent the Chancellor, i.e. the Leader of the Nazis, and to take charge of all matters concerning industrial peace, in particular questions of wage-rates. They were expressly bound to the policy of the government, and were inaugurated for a period " until the reorganisation of the social constitution ". Commentators of various types, Catholics and radical National-Socialists, saw in the institution of the Labour Trustees the assertion of a dangerous principle, a definite step towards the disfranchisement of the working-class. It should be the aim of the Corporate State to give each Corporation a large share in self-government. Through the Trustees, however, the workers were prevented from sharing the responsibility in matters which affected them most intimately—wages and working-conditions. The government said the measure was only temporary. Actually the Trustees have remained as one of the most characteristic features of National-Socialist society, and a law of January 20, 1934, perpetuates their existence.

During the first months of 1933 the Nazi leaders

tried to placate the working-class by words in order to make these structural changes more palatable. The economic condition of the workers was so desperate that any improvement in the standard of living would reconcile masses of the workers with the new regime. So, with the greatest noise, the Nazis in regional commands kept wages from falling and even, by threats, tried to keep employers from breaking wage-agreements. Much was talked of "Marxist" employers, and one or two managers were sent off to Concentration Camps for a few days. Although prices rose, owing to the government's tariff policy, sometimes an action was entered on against shopkeepers who charged "usurious" prices—in Munich a number of such shopkeepers were consigned one fine day to the Concentration Camp for a short spell. On the whole, after April, wage-rates ceased the catastrophic fall of 1932. No doubt the authoritative way in which Nazi factory-cell leaders spoke to managers instilled a belief into some of the workers that things would get better—though even this changed thoroughly after the Labour Trustees were put in charge, and finally ceased when Factory Councils were reorganised in 1934.[1] The

[1] An example of Nazi factory work was given the author by a worker (non-party) in a South German town. In May 1933 he was, as before, treasurer of his union-branch. He would go every pay-day to the local Nazi headquarters of the Labour Front to pay in the men's subscriptions, always at the same time of day. Once, as soon as he appeared, a Nazi official caught up the telephone, rang up the owner of the worker's factory, and read him a furious lesson concerning the wage-rates at the factory—particularly those of young workers. The affair was obviously staged. Nothing changed at the factory.

continual threats concerning overtime and wage-rates were, however, largely without effect—they were soon replaced by threats from governmental quarters against unwarranted interference in the industrial system. Much of it was no doubt honestly meant by the Nazi rank and file, for continual inner-Party friction has resulted. Many Storm Troopers have been excluded from the Party and consigned to Concentration Camps ; local Nazi organisations have been disbanded and purged. The Nazis who broke down the workers' organisations have found that there is now but one power, one organisation, one Press in Germany.

The Political Parties

Since the advent of Brüning to power, and especially since his fall, the development of German history had slipped more and more out of the framework of the political Parties ; the social alignment, the struggle between classes of society, had openly become decisive. Once Hitler had suppressed the Communist Party, dismissed the militant workers in the factories, and smashed the working-class organisations, the Trade Unions, there followed quite easily the dissolution or " co-ordination " of the old political Parties. Most of the forms of democracy went into voluntary, painless liquidation.

Social-Democracy had sealed its fate by its whole function during the Weimar Republic, through its recognition that the working-class must bow before the exigences of the whole of the State. Even when thousands of its officials were being maltreated, thrown into Concentration Camps, murdered, it refused to take on an illegal existence as an absolute negation of the National-Socialist State. On March 18 such of the Party as had not fled or been imprisoned appeared in the *Reichstag* as an honourable Opposition. Here its last act of defiance took place—it refused to vote for the Enabling Act: but it was an act of resigned and passive defiance, not of challenging struggle. There was personal bravery there, to vote against Hitler in a Chamber filled with armed Storm Troops—but it was an abdication of working-class struggle against Hitler. This was even more evident when the Parliamentary fraction voted confidence in Hitler's foreign policy on May 17—at a time when the Trade Unions had already been dissolved.

Such an open affirmation of Hitlerism could not take place without dissensions within the leadership of the Party. To some extent a rough cleavage of tactics was caused by the fact of exile. Some of the leaders, like Löbe and Severing, remained within Germany and were more conciliatory in their tactics; others, who had fled, like Wels, were on the whole for more energetic measures, for the construction of an illegal Party apparatus, of an illegal Press, etc. Even amongst the exiles, however, attempts were made at first to curry favour with Hitler. At a special session of the Second International, Wels refused to endorse the resolutions against Hitler, and actually resigned from that body (March 30). Later he declared that his resignation had merely been a demonstrative step, in order to spare his comrades in Germany from a harsher terror; when it was seen that his act had had no effect on Hitler, he rejoined the International. Whatever his intentions, a more incompetent policy, a more injurious act in the eyes of the working-class, could hardly be imagined. At a moment when the Terror against the working-class was at its height, Social-Democracy was more intent on begging Hitler for mercy than on leading the counter-struggle. The National-Socialists rightly judged these tactics as a confession of weakness, and on May 10 Göring occupied all Party-rooms in Prussia, and confiscated all Party newspapers and funds.

Within Germany several times new Central Committees of the Social-Democratic Party were elected, the last one on June 19, with Löbe, the most conciliatory of all, at its head. This Committee issued a strong condemnation of the Prague leadership, with its more militant policy. But even this did not help. On June 22 Frick issued a general prohibition of the Social-Democratic Party ; its members were excluded from all representative and elected bodies ; its newspapers were prohibited in permanence. The four members of the Central Committee were imprisoned, one, Stelling, being killed. On July 14 the whole Party property was confiscated. All its wavering and manœuvring had only discredited it in the eyes of its former members and the working-class in general.

The behaviour of individual leaders of the Party is not of great political significance. Some acted bravely and paid the penalty. Others, like Otto Braun, formerly Premier of Prussia, ran away from responsibilities and slipped across the frontier in good time. Others again went over to Hitler, like Löbe. But the collapse of the Social-Democratic Party is not a matter of personalities. Its rôle as mediator between workers and State was played out. The State had decided that the working-class could no longer be allowed to have its own organs ; the class-struggle had shown itself in its crassest form. But Social-Democracy had denied the class-struggle.[1] It had no further basis of existence in Hitler's Germany.

The Democratic Parties, the State Party and the People's Party, had disappeared to all intents and purposes at the March elections—no terror was necessary to make their supporters and leaders go over to the Hitler-Hugenberg camp. The Catholic Centre too, though maintaining most of its support in the elections, had really abdicated with the completion of Brüning's policy, when he was abandoned by the big interests. For the *Reichstag* of March 18 the vote of the Centre was still formally important, as only with its support could Hitler gain the necessary majority to pass his Enabling Act. On Hitler's promise that he would respect the rights of the Catholic Church—like many others, a promise Hitler has not kept—the Catholics gave him their vote. It meant the complete acceptance of National-Socialism, and caused serious dissensions in the Party, many of the Catholic workers turning against their leaders. The leader of the Party, Dr. Kaas, re-

[1] Cf. Mr. George Lansbury in *The Clarion*, May 5, 1934 : " We must organise against the Class War."

signed. Brüning was elected into his place, and immediately entered into negotiations with Hitler. But while the central leadership of the Party came close to Hitler, its resistance grew in the provinces. The separatism of the Party, strong under Bismarck, became more prominent, so much so that the Nazis undertook a violent campaign against the Catholic Bavarian People's Party, destroying its property and breaking up its meetings. On July 5 the Centre Party proclaimed its own dissolution, this being ratified in the Concordat ; though for the time the Catholic Church preserved its own Youth and Cultural movements.

The German Nationalist Party was apparently in a much stronger position, with its preponderance of Ministerial posts. Its weakness relative to the National-Socialist Party was, however, doubly evident—in its lack of mass-support, and in the confusion and contradictions in its own leadership. It had never been able to unite fully the preponderant industrial interests, nor the great landowners. In the stress of the Crisis the contradictions in its own ranks had grown sharper, industrialists and landowners had fallen away to Hitlerism. The result of this was an inefficient vacillation in home and foreign policy. On the one hand, the old reactionary methods were dangerous. The attempt at forming Company Unions failed, as we have seen ; it failed to make allowance for the great unrest in the working-class. The monarchist aims of the Party were too openly indicative of a pro-Junker policy. As Minister for Agriculture Hugenberg succeeded in rescuing landowners from compulsory bankruptcy, and in lowering interest rates to 4½ per cent. But here he failed to mobilise opinion round his Bill, and was mercilessly attacked by National-Socialist demagogy, which proclaimed that 4½ per cent was too high. On the other hand, Hugenberg and his like tried to incorporate National-Socialist methods and slogans in their policy, but made serious errors. When Hugenberg tried to pander to the demagogic tastes of the Nazis by presenting, at the World Economic Conference, a memorandum proposing the colonisation of the Ukraine, he simply succeeded in alarming the world against Hitler-Germany.

These tactical mistakes weaned the powerful interests away from the German Nationalist Party. But it had its own fighting organisation, the Steel Helmets, and these formed a force which, possessing arms and the traditional support of the Army, had to be dealt with diplomatically. The first step here was that Seldte, the Steel Helmet leader, was made Minister of Labour. His Second-in-Command, Duesterberg, was got rid of on the grounds of a Non-Aryan grandmother. The Steel Helmets were incorporated in only modest proportions in the Auxiliary Police, and on April 27 Seldte put himself under the command of Röhm, the chief of the Nazi Storm Troops. The Steel Helmets tried to resist by taking into their ranks many oppositional elements, notably Social-Democrats, who saw in the Steel Helmets an organisation which would be able to fight against Hitler. This provoked violent attacks from the Nazis. The groups of Steel Helmets were compulsorily purged.

Later even the name Steel Helmets was abandoned, and was replaced by the National-Socialist Front Soldiers' League ; together with this a great campaign of propaganda was carried out by the government against the Reaction, by which the Steel Helmets and the German Nationalists were meant. In June 1934 Seldte was actually stoned by young Nazis.

Though there was much disaffection in the ranks of Steel Helmets, some showing sympathy even for Communists, the power of the organisation as an independent military force was broken. In June 1933 the German Nationalists tried to form a stronger civil organisation, the *Kampfringe*, for carrying on active political and industrial agitation in the various districts. The Party, being hampered in its central activities, thus hoped to build up strong local organs. But in the middle of June these *Kampfringe* were violently dissolved by the Nazis. At the end of June Hugenberg, who received no support from Hindenburg as he had hoped, resigned his chairmanship of the Party. At the same time he was forced to resign from the Cabinet. On July 14 came the end : all political Parties but one were declared dissolved : " in Germany there is only one political Party, the National-Socialist German Workers' Party ".

Thus collapsed, ingloriously, out of inward impoverishment, the political forms of the democratic Republic. The reasons for the collapse of the " democratic " Parties are clear ; they become urgent from the beginning of the Crisis, and avow themselves with Brüning's regime. The Crisis set problems which could not be solved within the framework of the democratic Republic. These problems were economic and social ; to salvage German economy, German capitalism, far-reaching blows had to be dealt at the class which resisted the changes necessary. The working-class had to be forced—or " moulded ", as some Nazis hoped—to the necessities of the situation. The democratic Parties, including Social-Democracy, acquiesced in this forcing of the workers ; by doing so they forfeited their birthright. They abdicated what political liberties they possessed as a necessary consequence of the withdrawal of like liberties from the workers. For, in every country, the measure of political liberty is the liberty assured to the working-class.

It was necessary too that the undemocratic, reactionary German-Nationalist Party should be dissolved. This was not so much because this Party pointed to pre-War conditions as ideal—even the Nazis view Bismarck as a hero. But, since the Crisis, the masses in Germany demanded a reform which would affect them personally, a reform in which they personally would participate. Though in the National-Socialist movement they created a highly undemocratic instrument, they yet felt it to be the means of breaking down the old clique of State leaders, of big interests—it was not without reason that Goebbels, on the occasion of the plebiscite concerning Germany's withdrawal from the League of Nations, tried to point out the *democratic* nature of the German government (November 1933). National-Socialism was going to set free the masses, economically from the control of the big capitalists, politically from foreign oppression and from parliamentary cliques. In this sense it spoke to the masses, flattered them, cajoled them, gave them the illusion of power of the Storm Troops. The German-Nationalist Party did none of these things. It promised to do away with democratic forms only that the big interests might rule naked and unashamed. It allowed for no political, no *emotional* participation of the masses in the government. There was an underlying similarity of policy between it and Hitlerism ; but its tactics were wrong and dangerous for its cause. Thus its own backers abandoned it, and saw it die without regret. It renounced a seeming liberty for a real kingdom, as we shall now see.

CHAPTER IX

THE ECONOMIC STRUCTURE OF THE NATIONAL-SOCIALIST STATE

Industry

The reconstruction of German economic life began with the National-Socialist revolution; or rather, the revolution was a part of the reconstruction of German economy. Two sharply opposed policies were evident within industrial circles under the Republic, the differences between which became more and more irreconcilable as the crisis grew in severity. One was the Fulfilment policy, recognising foreign obligations in return for foreign financial help, building Germany's prosperity on foreign capital; shirking as much as possible further demands for "national" efforts and economies for fear of the resistance with which they would be met from the working-classes. The other policy, the most prominent mouthpiece of which was Schacht, set its face against further indebtedness, and looked for an internal reorganisation to overcome Germany's weakness; and this reorganisation meant the imposition of great burdens on the German people, meant the crushing of all bodies, political and social, which would oppose additional burdens. The problem of German agriculture was, for the adherents of Fulfilment, mainly a social problem, a problem of unemployment and indebtedness ; for the aggressive nationalists it was a political problem, a problem of national self-sufficiency in time of war. Hitlerism was the political aspect of this latter policy.

These two policies stood in opposition in all spheres of political and economic life. In the heart of German economy, in the huge Steel Trust and its allied concerns, it came more and more to an open conflict as production and shares fell, as disaster overcame subsidiary enterprises. Otto Wolff, one of the largest shareholders, represented the policy of conciliation. He aimed at consolidating the industry by an alliance with foreign, above all French, capital. With the powerful backing of the *Deutsche Bank* he entered into dealings with French heavy industry, and was already linked up with Luxembourg industry. Thyssen, his opponent, schemed to break the control of foreign capital, to conquer the world economically instead of being forced into an unequal compromise. He was ready to challenge foreign capital, to repudiate Germany's debts, and to profit by the ensuing international tension and war preparations. Otto Wolff worked in close conjunction with Catholic interests on the Rhine, and found in Brüning a worthy representative. Thyssen, on the other hand, saw that his policy needed a new social and economic organisation of Germany. Of all the great industrialists it was he who encouraged and supported Hitler most actively, carrying on propaganda and collecting those immense funds on which National-Socialism fed.

The advent of Hitler to power was the signal of the victory of Thyssen over the Otto Wolff group. The Anti-Semitic campaign was utilised to get rid of Wolff's ally, Oscar Wassermann, the chairman of the *Deutsche Bank*, and to undermine the position of Wolff's partners, Othmar Strauss and Silverberg. A year later Wolff himself lost his directorate of the *Deutsche Bank*. Thyssen then, with the aid of Schacht, set out to organise German industry in such a way that his own power became dominant. He effected a widening of the Steel Trust so that the majority of the State, gained by Brüning's transactions in 1932, was turned into a small minority. Some of his own almost insolvent concerns were joined with the Steel Trust, so that in the new form of the Steel Trust Thyssen himself owns 18 per cent of the shares, and is the largest private shareholder instead of the third. Through his close connexion with the National-Socialist movement Thyssen was given administrative control over the State's shares, amounting to 22 per cent, and is thus virtual lord of the Steel Trust. Otto Wolff has sunk to comparative insignificance through these manipulations, owning only 9 per cent of the stock. Parallel with this, Thyssen became in July 1933 chairman of the two strongest employers' federations in the Rhineland—the *Langnamverein* and the *Gruppe Nordwest*.[1]

Mere economic control was not sufficient for Thyssen and his allies. They had to secure administrative and political power. A first step was the

[1] For further details of the ramifications of Thyssen's power, see Ernst Henri, *Hitler over Europe?* Dent, 1934, Chap. I.

abolition of the old National Economic Council, on which employees and the lower middle-class were represented. A Provisional Economic Council was nominated on April 5, which is still in existence. The industrialist Krupp von Bohlen is president, and its composition is as follows: four bankers, nine representatives of Big Industry, two great landlords, and, as sole " representative " of the working-class, Dr. Ley, the leader of the Labour Front.

The more radical of the National-Socialists tried to check this consolidation of the power of industry and banks, but all their efforts only resulted in giving it a disguise. Otto Wagener, the Nazi specialist for economic affairs, attempted to harness the employers to the National-Socialist movement. He put National-Socialists into key-positions in the State Federation of Industry (*Reichsverband der deutschen Industrie*). For the moment he even achieved the resignation of Krupp as chairman of the Federation, and put in one of his own nominees. In June Wagener went farther and made preparations for the creation of a Corporation of German Industry on which workers' representatives would sit together with employers. But this was going too far. His reforms had taken place while Hugenberg was Minister for Industry. In June Schmitt, a recent convert to National-Socialism and chairman of the biggest German insurance company, became Minister in Hugenberg's place. He immediately removed Wagener from his Party post, and Wagener's nominees on the Federation lost their jobs. Wilhelm Keppler, the manager of an engineering works with a long practical business experience, took Wagener's place. With this change all idea of uniting workers and employers in one Corporation is abandoned. As Ley said, National-Socialism is to create, not the Corporate State, but the National-Socialist State—a tautology which has meaning enough. Krupp was restored to his position as chairman of the Employers' Federation, which characteristically retains the name of State Corporation of Industry, although it is simply and solely a federation of employers. This devolution of National-Socialist radicalism has its exact parallel in the collapse of the onslaught on the Big Stores.[1]

Thyssen went farther to establish his own grip on German industry. Göring, the Premier of Prussia, appointed him State Councillor, and invested him with plenary powers in the whole industrial area of Westphalia and the Ruhr. All economic matters in this district, the most important in all Germany, were put unreservedly in his charge. The National-Socialist leaders of the district published a declaration of absolute loyalty and obedience to him. In the November *Reichstag* elections his own candidates headed the Party lists for the area—his managing director Vögler, later to become leader of one of the main groups of German industry, his associate Springorum, a steel magnate and director of the *Deutsche Bank*, these were the local candidates of the National-Socialist Party. Göring took an economic adviser, Tengelmann, the son of the general manager of one of Thyssen's concerns. Flick, Thyssen's old

[1] See pp. 189–199.

ally, was given control over the industry of Middle Germany.

But the National-Socialist revolution was not merely a private gain of Thyssen's, no more than the Inflation had been a private gain of Stinnes's. It was the victory of aggressive Heavy Industry, which thus cut the Gordian Knot of its problems. It was not aiming at winning places of honour, but at removing the obstacles to its prosperity. The Trade Unions were broken, to be replaced in all administrative functions by the Trustees of Labour, officials nominated by the State who were to settle all differences between masters and men. The Factory Councils were done away with, the employers becoming " masters in their own house ". All the political organisations of the working-class were suppressed. The way was clear for a reorganisation of German economy according to the principles of big industry. The first and decisive step in its constructive programme, after it had secured the necessary administrative posts, was the law on Compulsory Cartellisation of July 15, by which the whole of German industry was to come under the direct surveillance of the big interests.

The most important of German industries were highly trustified or cartellised even before Hitler came to power. Since before the War there had existed Syndicates of coal and potash supervised by the State, to which all producers had been forced to belong, and which had fixed quotas and prices for the various enterprises. On April 21 these Syndicates were reformed so as to give less power to the workers employed in these industries and so as to centralise control. Through Thyssen's manipulations the Steel Trust had become more comprehensive. The electrical industry was practically trustified in the Siemens group, and in other industries, such as the film industry, monopoly-groups dominated the production. In many industries cartels had existed —over a thousand in the period of the Republic— but their position was not satisfactory for the cartel-members. Outsiders could always challenge the cartel, the cartels in the throes of the crisis threatened to fall to pieces and to give way to fierce price-warfare. In many cases rival cartels were at each other's throats, as in the cable and paper industries. The law of Compulsory Cartellisation was to put an end to all this. The government gave itself the power to force all similar enterprises to form a cartel, the aims of which would be the fixing of prices, the apportionment of fixed quotas to every firm, the prohibition of the expansion of business and of the establishment of new firms. No firms were allowed to remain outside such a cartel. Severe punishments were threatened against all firms which should break the cartel-agreements.

So far more than twenty industries have been cartellised under this law, including the glass, wire, jute, soap, paper, hardware, china, cigarette, starch, salt, brass, chocolate and sweets, clothing, rubber-tyre, and wireless-receiver industries. The general principle is that the State, while compelling the industries to form the cartel, shall not itself be represented on the cartel, shall not play an "inorganic" part in business, as it is put. Its power is voluntarily restricted to the examination and approval of prices and to a power of intervention where necessary. The policy of the cartel is in the hands of the manufacturers themselves, and the biggest share of control belongs to the biggest firms. The immediate effect is to bolster up prices. The index-figure for wholesale prices of industrial raw materials and half-finished goods for the foreign market were, from July 1933 to June 1934, on the average 66·4; for the home market 103·6. Governmental pronouncements are made to the effect that prices will not be affected by the cartellisation; but it is significant how much polemic is devoted by leaders of industry to the question of price-cutting, "the silliest of all commercial malpractices", as the director of the State Combine of the clothing industry called it.

The cartel has the two aims of the elimination of competition and the fixing of a "just" price. The former aim is directly opposed to the mass of National-Socialist propaganda which was calculated to attract the "small man". Though in the National-Socialist State criticism cannot be open, murmurs have been heard reminding the Party of its former policy. A leading article in the Party organ, the *Völkischer Beobachter* of March 22, remarks that after the formation of the Potash Syndicate in 1910, "the aim of the various Potash firms in the Syndicate was not, as in other branches of industry, to win new markets or to develop cheaper and better forms of production, but to gain a bigger quota of the whole Potash production, especially as influence in the Syndicate was dependent on the size of the quota."

The chief activity within a cartel is bound to be the scheming between the bigger interests for financial control over the smaller firms. This is already happening in some of the new cartels, the large interests lending capital to the weaker brethren to "strengthen" them. And already difficulties have arisen in more than one industry over the quotas, the small firms complaining that they had not received their due (cf. the complaints of Dresden cigarette factories, which led to the resignation of the chairman of the cigarette cartel).[1]

In industrial circles few voices are raised against the principle of the "just price", as it is euphemistically called. All the big interests long for a fixed price and its guarantee of security and power. A timid but unconvincing reprimand comes from the *Frankfurter Zeitung* of April 6. The relative costs of production in similar types of factories are here compared, on the basis of official figures, and it is pointed out that costs vary astonishingly, the same process costing in some factories two or three times as much as in others. The conclusion is that there can be no question of a "just price", nor can one talk recklessly of malicious price-cutting. This article, belonging to a forgotten liberal age, is ignored in Germany. It shows, however, that the price-fixing of the cartels, while assuring profit to all firms, will take away the incentive to technical progress, and will, in more ways than one, weaken Germany's position on the world-market.

The cartel-policy has repercussions in many spheres

[1] *Frankfurter Zeitung*, May 26.

of German economic life. In the soap industry, after a good deal of resistance from some firms, the cartel was formed. Prices were fixed on the basis of the compulsory use of German tallow, the price of which is considerably higher than foreign. The cartel is, hence, being used to strengthen German self-sufficiency. Again, in the china cartel, after prices had been fixed, tradesmen made a protest against raising the prices of the cheaper sorts of crockery, and tried to establish maximum prices, without success. And especially among the mass of the population there are continual complaints—one of the causes of the Party campaign against "Carpers and Grousers" in June 1934. The price of consumption goods has risen in a year from the index-figure of 109 to 115. The cost-of-living figures give an increase of food prices by 4·3 per cent, of clothing by 4·2 per cent between June 1933 and June 1934; on the other hand, the turnover in retail sales dropped from the index-figure of 66 in 1932 (1928 = 100), to 60 in 1933, and still stands at approximately this latter figure. While dividends and profits are uniformly improving, the situation of the lower classes, and of the traders who depend on their power of consumption, is growing steadily worse.

Corresponding to the cartellisation within industry the National-Socialist State is carrying through a reorganisation of employers' federations which is to put industry under the centralised control of the powerful interests. On February 27 the Minister for Trade and Industry was given power to organise all industrial and commercial federations under a leadership responsible directly to the State. He was given power to break up or strengthen any existing federations, to dismiss their chairmen, to put in his own nominees. He could force all firms to join the federations. Kessler, the National-Socialist expert for economic affairs,[1] was put in charge of this reorganisation, and so far industry has been divided up into 13 main Groups, each divided into subgroups. These Groups are to have in their competence all general questions affecting the industries. They link up with the Provisional Economic Council, and like it, are led by the biggest interests. For instance, the leader of Group 10—for Banks and Finance—is the banker Otto Fischer ; and as leader of the sub-group Private Joint Stock Banks he nominates Friedrich Reinhart, a director of the *Commerz und Privat Bank* ; as leader of the sub-group Private Banks the banker Schröder ; as leader of the subgroup Private Mortgage Banks Schreyer, a director of the Bavarian Mortgage Bank. Main Group 4, for engineering, has as its leader Vögler, Thyssen's managing director. The leader of Group 2 for iron and metal goods is Hartkopf, director of the famous Solingen steel works, and president of the Essen Chamber of Commerce, etc. etc.

In the same way the export trade in general is being organised under the leadership of Dr. Lüer, a National-Socialist, who is president of the Frankfurt Chamber of Commerce and was Trustee of

[1] Kessler was removed from his post in July 1934, for being too dilatory.

Labour for the Frankfurt district. As a preparatory step detail reports are demanded from all exporters as to what and how much they export. It has been proposed that quotas will be imposed on exports. Very bitter recriminations have been levelled at firms exporting under the normal price. The difficulties in the way of this cartellisation of export are enormous, since German prices are already too high to compete with foreign producers, and Germany is losing its old markets to foreigners. This was emphasised at the Congress of Hamburg Export Trade on April 19, in a speech by Reyss, a director of Siemens-Schuckert. It seems that the export trade looks to the State for subsidies. But here again we find the dominant note, the big interests control the organisation. Reyss, in the speech mentioned above, suggests that the small trader be cut out, and that the great producers organise export themselves. If German export is rescued, it will be at the expense of the small man.

Industry in Hitler-Germany is trustified through and through. Point 13 of the Party Programme, which demanded the nationalisation of trusts, is wretchedly betrayed. What of the banks, which were so scathingly trounced by Nazi demagogy?

In the Summer of 1933 a Commission was appointed to investigate the German banking system and propose remedies to reform it in the spirit of National-Socialism. At the end of the year, Schacht, the chairman of this Commission, announced that they had come to the conclusion that " nationalisation of the banks could not be recommended ".

Some mutterings were heard, complaints that the members of the Commission were the old gang of bankers who had sat on all the financial committees of the Republic. But Goebbels's organ, *Der Angriff*, expressed itself satisfied, and Schmitt, the Minister for Trade, energetically declared that all theoretical discussions concerning the lowering of interest must cease. Schacht finally chased away all fears by stating, on February 22, 1934, at the Banking Conference, that the government had no intention of using violent measures. And private bankers like Schröder were given charge over the organisation of the banking Groups.

The principle of Leadership is no mere moral idea, as it is enunciated by the Nazi leaders. It has its reality in the economic sphere. It means, all power to the big interests. Cartel-policy is governed by the greatest and most powerful members of the Cartel. The basic principles of the Cartel are the elimination of competition, the guarantee of the existing economic powers. As a secondary line of defence the big interests have the system of governmental Groups. The Leaders of these Groups have not to interfere in Cartel affairs except where necessary. But, if it does become necessary, they can step in. And these Leaders are all members of the big concerns, of the biggest businesses and banks. When their interference is, in their opinion, necessary, they can apply in their cause the whole weight of State authority. This is the result of National-Socialist principles. The process which Marx defined, by which industry becomes ever more monopolistic, receives through National-Socialism a sudden, ruthless impetus. The National-Socialist State is the State of Monopoly-Capital.

Agriculture

The agricultural policy of National-Socialism does not stand in quite so harsh a contrast to their professions as does their industrial policy. While the principle of profit, and of profit to the big interests, dominates all their acts on the industrial field, in agriculture other principles come to the fore. Dr. Lüer, speaking at Bremen on April 12 at the Congress of the Export Trade, mentioned the "great sacrifices" which the country was making for the sake of agriculture. "The peasantry is the basis of the State." Some defence of the government's agricultural policy was necessary for exporters, whose prices are forced up by the high prices of agricultural produce in Germany. A closer definition of the reasons for the "sacrifices" was given in September 1933 by Meinberg, Darré's Deputy in the Agricultural Corporation. He stated that a strong peasantry must be built up, particularly in East Germany, as a military and economic force to protect German frontiers. For the National-Socialist government, the agricultural question is predominantly a political one, and only secondarily an economic problem, and the social reorganisation of agriculture follows on this political line. Military and economic considerations here fall together. Germany must become self-sufficient in the production of foodstuffs; and the countryside must, from a strategical point of view, have strong centres round which the ruling-class can organise resistance to the invader.

One of the questions uppermost in the minds of the peasantry who voted National-Socialist was, What would Hitler do with the heavily indebted large estates? These estates had absorbed millions of marks from the *Osthilfe* subsidy. Their insolvency caused impoverishment and unemployment to the land-workers. They had not enough capital to buy machinery and organise on a modern basis. Much of Nazi propaganda had demanded and promised the break-up of these estates, and the setting free of the land for independent settlers and peasants. Would Darré, made Minister for Agriculture in June, carry out this plan?

Though the National-Socialist Party called itself the Party of the peasantry, in its upper circles there were few peasants, but many landowners, many officers of the landowning class, the traditional nursery of army officers. Of the 288 National-Socialists elected to the *Reichstag* in March 1933, 33 were officers, 21 big landowners, and 22 big farmers; apart from all other support, this meant that 26·4 per cent of the Party group was in favour of a policy advantageous to the big landowners. Similarly, of the 160 leaders of the Nazi Party, mentioned in the book *Pictures of our Leaders*, an official Party publication of 1931, 36 are officers and landowners, a percentage of 22·5. Apart from the urgent need to satisfy this strong group in the Party, the strategical importance of the large estates in time of war had to be considered. While a land populated with small peasantry is not particularly suitable for military defence, a land of large estates is the opposite. As the experience of the War of Liberation of 1813–14 showed, the estates of the nobles can serve as rallying grounds for the people. Having the position of leadership in economy, the landowners naturally assume the political leadership over the smaller fry. To break the backbone of the landowning class would be to weaken Germany's military strength.

It was considerations like these which brought Darré to express opinions which were a cold douche to the hopes of many Nazis. In a memorable speech of the 19th of July 1933, he stated : "I will not lay hands on any estate, however large, if it be economically sound. . . . I will also not lay hands on any indebted large estate, but leave it to struggle along as best it may." Indeed, Darré has done much to put these indebted estates into a sounder position, giving them along with the whole of agriculture a guaranteed market. Some attempt was made to persuade them to give up part of their land in payment of debts, but this method of liquidation of their debts was in no way forced on them, and has had practically no result.

Darré's most grandiose scheme was the Hereditary Estate Law (*Erbhofgesetz*). This served the double purpose of preserving their estates to the nobility, and of building up a well-to-do peasantry in place of the small peasant. It was proclaimed as giving back to the peasantry their traditional rights, taken from them at the dawn of liberalism, when the peasants were freed and thrown on to the labour market. The precise aim of the *Erbhofgesetz*, decreed on September 29, was to protect agricultural estates from being split up and dissolved by debts or inheritance. This economic measure is to establish as the basis of the social order in the countryside a solid class of permanent, well-to-do or wealthy landowners. The *Erbhof* is to be permanent and hereditary. However big the mortgages on an estate, the unit called the hereditary estate cannot be expropriated. The peasant is not allowed to divide up his inheritance among his children, but must leave his *Erbhof* to one heir. But, as I have said, the law had a double purpose. The size of an *Erbhof* may be anything from a small unit just sufficient to nourish a family to an estate of 125 hectares (500 acres).[1] If not mortgaged to more than 30 per cent of their taxable value, the large estates can be divided up into a number of estates of 500 acres, these assigned to their owners (the family of the landowner), and declared inalienable. Thus the indebted large landowners are rescued finally from the threat of bankruptcy. And when we find, in present-day Germany, that nobles inscribe themselves as " peasants ", it is not evidence of a revolution in feeling, but of economic expediency. Non-Aryans are not allowed to possess an *Erbhof*.

The law has implications which are pregnant with strife in the future. There is the purely financial difficulty of getting credit for the owners of the hereditary estates. Now that the banks may not

[1] This maximum of 500 acres has already been frequently exceeded, e.g. in Hanover.

expropriate the estates, they are chary of giving loans. They can lend money either in the trust that agriculture will prosper and the peasant be honest, or on the security of that part of the peasant's property which does not belong properly to the *Erbhof*. The reluctance of the banks has already called forth governmental protests and schemes for developing co-operative banking still further, though this also is not simple on the basis of the law.[1]

A more serious drawback is the social conflict called forth by the law. While a class of big peasantry is being formed, which will be a powerful conservative force, at the same time a large class of agricultural proletarians is growing in the place of independent and semi-independent peasants. While one son or brother inherits the whole of the patrimonial estate, the rest of the family is left without means, and has only the " right " of being employed on the *Erbhof* as labourers. Usually the younger sons are proletarianised, while the heir inclines to the ranks of the middle-class. The class-war, which has in the recent past been less sharp on the land than in the towns, is being given a crude reality which will lead to severe struggles in the future. At the moment great efforts are being made to absorb the peasants expropriated by the *Erbhofgesetz* by land-settlement. They are given the first option on reclaimed land. But this, even if possible for a short

[1] Darré said in a speech at Munich, April 22, that the peasants should not grumble at the difficulty of getting credit, as this was the way to break the " bondage of interest ". If one is forbidden to borrow, then one will never have creditors !

time, cannot cope with the constant stream of dispossessed peasants which the *Erbhofgesetz* pours into the land. The strengthening of agricultural capitalism means the strengthening of the agricultural proletariat.

The chief economic task of the National-Socialists in agriculture was to secure the home market for home produce, and to make Germany as far as possible self-sufficient in agricultural raw materials. Some headway was made by Hugenberg's law for the liquidation of agricultural debts (June 1, 1933). Banking operations were set in motion to convert all debts into loans at not more than 4½ per cent. Big estates were given a chance to offer land in part-payment of their debts—though this remained a fairly dead clause. Small-holders who had settled on the land since 1930 were given a moratorium of two years on the interest-payments of their debts, provided that they paid back the principal in instalments. Special loans were put at the disposal of agriculture by the State for repairs to farm-buildings, machines, etc., and tax-rebates were granted for money spent in equipping farms. Farm-labourers were taken out of the Unemployment Insurance, so that overhead charges dropped considerably for the larger farms.

But all these financial measures only cleared the ground. German agriculture, owing to methods of working and tenure, rents, taxation-burdens, could still not compete with foreign. The National-Socialist government provided the necessary impetus by a policy of self-sufficiency, carrying Von Papen's system of quotas to its logical conclusion. Nearly all staple agricultural foodstuffs have a guaranteed market, cereals, eggs, butter, etc. In some cases imports are completely forbidden—this also with the intention of stopping the export of German gold. At the same time prices are fixed by the State. The effect on prices has been strongly marked. Foodstuffs are in the retail shops far more expensive than in 1932. Particularly the staple food of the poor has been affected. The price of potatoes rose from April 1933 to April 1934 by 15 per cent, butter by 28 per cent, margarine by 38 per cent, eggs by 15 per cent. Sugar rose slightly, being already far higher than the 1929 price.[1] It was this rise in the cost of living which to some extent made the rigid protectionist and monopolist policy in industry essential, as the question of dropping wages to make competition with foreign products possible became a more and more serious social measure. And while in some cases the small as well as big agriculturists gained, in others the small peasants were injured. The prohibition of the import of oil-seeds served the interests only of the greater farmers, and meant an increase in the price of cattle-food. Or again, the quotas for potato spirit show that 82 per cent is allotted to the large distilleries, the rest to the small and medium-sized ones.

The law of Compulsory Cartellisation of July 15 applied to agriculture as well as industry, and has resulted in a series of regulations. Amongst other things, milk, eggs, cereals, fats, hops, cattle for slaughter, milling, spirit from potato distilleries, wool,

[1] The German wholesale price (June 1934) for butter is 2½ times, for eggs nearly twice, for pork 1½ times, for sugar four times as high as in England.

are subject to this law. Prices are fixed and quotas apportioned. What is left over cannot be sold. The general form is that in every district, in some cases in every village, depots or markets are established, to which the producers bring their produce. Trading Associations, under State supervision, or licensed traders, then take charge of the sale to the consumers. Often there is a startlingly large gap between the price paid to the producers and that paid to the State by the consumers. The peasant may get 4–5 pfennigs per egg, but the price to the consumer is 8–10 pfennigs. There have already been numerous cases of peasants trying to sabotage the quotas, the police making raids on the markets and fining numbers of unlicensed traders at a time. The producers are told bluntly by the government that if they have a surplus over their quota, they can use it for household consumption or give it to the pigs.[1]

In order to provide a centralised executive for the carrying out of this reorganisation, all agricultural federations and leagues have been absorbed into the Agricultural Corporation. This has its own national " Peasant Leader ", with officials in all districts. This " Corporation " deserves the name almost as little as does the Corporation of Industry. It is true, land-workers are included in it. But they have no representation of their own. The leaders are all nominated by the Minister for Agriculture, and the

[1] An article in the *Kölnische Zeitung* (July 18, 1934) compares the present fixed-price system to that imposed during the War. The hope is expressed that the illegal trading common then will be prevented now by the " changed outlook " in the peasants.

agricultural proletariat has absolutely no means of expressing, let alone realising its will. Its resentment, just as the resentment of the smaller peasantry, finds expression at present in that subterranean grumbling which is causing the National-Socialist Party so much worry. There is, just as always in the liberal age, a constant tendency to leave the land and find work in the towns, owing to the better wages and conditions there, owing to the lack of Unemployment insurance on the land. This the government is trying to prevent by a series of decrees prohibiting land-workers from leaving the land. Many aspects of serfdom are emerging again, and a rumble of revolt is echoing through the land.

The system of fixed prices and quotas on the land can be dubbed " national planning ". How does it compare with planning in Soviet Russia ? We have seen how, in industry, German planning is associated fundamentally with *restriction* of production, with prohibitions against expansion of businesses, prohibitions even against the use of certain types of labour-saving machinery.[1] On the land the same principle is at work. The abandonment of " free " economy means the " screwing-back " of production. Prices and quotas are fixed, in the official phrase, " according to general economic conditions and the power of consumption in the country ". This imprisons the national economy in a vicious circle. Instead of production being increased according to a prescribed plan, so that the wealth of the country increases at a fixed rate, the " power of consumption " is made

[1] e.g. in the cigarette industry.

the fixed economic constant which determines production. But wages, owing to lowness of production and the need for profit, do not rise, but consistently fall. As a result, quotas or prices have to drop. The vital principle of National-Socialist "planning" is that prices are fixed; and therefore production is more and more restricted. The only exception to this is the production of goods valuable for military purposes. In agriculture there is a small exception in the policy of developing land-settlement, which would naturally increase agricultural production. But it is noticeable that, in spite of the National-Socialist propaganda for land-settlement as a means of absorbing unemployment, the area of land settled in 1933 was only half as large as that in 1931 and 1932, and the work of preparing land for settlement has to be done by the labour-service, at slave-labour rates of pay.

The Small Tradesmen

Statistics concerning the social composition of Hitler's supporters are wanting. On the whole one can only deduce from the programmes and activity of the National-Socialist Party in its period of struggle what classes of society formed its main forces. The Programme, maintaining the principle of free capitalistic competition, and at the same time demanding State-control of big enterprises and banks, reflects chiefly the outlook of the lower middle-class, small business men, shopkeepers, artisans, peasants, etc. These formed the core of the rank and file of the Storm Troopers, together with those sections of the population whose occupation brings them into close touch with them, for instance shop-assistants, clerks, etc. During the crisis desperate elements from the unemployed proletariat joined up, though still relatively small numbers from the workers in big industry, where Socialist and Communist organisation and aims were strong. The professional classes, when unemployed, flocked to Hitler's troops. In particular it is very noticeable how many former officers, from the Army, Navy, and Air Force, played a leading part in Hitler's movement.[1] We need only mention Röhm, Göring, Von Epp, Von Levetzow, Hess (Hitler's deputy), Ley. To them came numerous desperadoes from the *Freikorps*, who carried on guerilla warfare against the Republic after 1918—Schulze, Heines, etc. These were the tacticians of the struggle ; but the stuff of the movement was the lower middle-class.

In the middle of 1933 a statistical investigation of the S.A. in two districts of Berlin was carried out (published in the Berlin *Nachtausgabe* of August 30). The results show fairly different results for East and West Berlin, and are worth reprinting[2] :

	S.A.	
	East Berlin. per cent.	West Berlin. per cent.
Working men	29	9
Artisans and technicians	44	33
Business men, assistants, shopkeepers, etc.	17	22
Officials and academic	2	16
Students	1	11
Other professions	7	9

[1] Ernst Henri gives an interesting account of the importance of these young retired officers in *Hitler Over Europe?* (Dents) pp. 246 ff.

[2] Taken from *Unsere Zeit* (Basle), September 1933.

From this table we can see that much more than half the Berlin S.A. is made up of lower middle-class elements. The percentage of working-men was also much higher in August 1933 than at the beginning of the year. In the elections to the Factory Councils the Nazis only began to make headway in March, during the terror. Their "conquest" of the proletariat took place on the basis of their political supremacy. The Storm Troops in their period of struggle before May 1933 were much more completely than later composed of lower middle-class elements.

The aim of the lower middle-class—if one may speak of such heterogeneous elements as a class—was its preservation. The force crushing it out of existence was large-scale enterprise. In the distributive trades Chain Stores, One-Price Stores, Big Stores were crushing the small shopkeeper out of existence. Artisans, small technicians, cobblers, small builders, were finding it impossible to com pete with highly capitalised, mechanised businesses. Mortgage laid its dead hand on the small businesses, and induced in them, in their desperate plight, a hatred for banks and finance-capital, which seemed effortlessly to suck their life-blood. But they feared also the proletariat. Socialism they conceived as directed against their own small possessions, as the negation of their ambition to rise economically and socially. The working-men's co-operatives took the trade of the small shops. Envy too crept in, for the proletariat had its own institutions, its insurance, its legal representatives, its organised party with its recognised place in the constitution of Germany.

The Storm Troops were the real military body of the lower middle-class. But within the National-Socialist Party it formed, too, its own economic organisation, one of the most significant of all the organisations of this period in Germany's history. It was led by Dr. von Renteln, former leader of the Hitler Youth, and was named the "Fighting League of the Trading Middle Class" (*Kampfbund für den gewerblichen Mittelstand*). The aim of this League was to control Germany's economic policy, within the framework of Hitlerism, to the advantage of the small traders and artisans, to preserve the hard-won independence of the industrious small man. It was largely its members who smashed the windows of the big stores, who insisted on the boycott of the Jewish stores, who demanded annihilating taxation on the big stores. It strove to realise Point 16 of the Party Programme—"municipal control of the big stores, which are to be rented at cheap prices to the small traders".

On March 28, 1933, this League won its first big victory by gaining control over the National Association of Retail Traders. It proceeded to form a National Corporation of Trade (*Reichsstand des deutschen Handels*) and a National Corporation of Artisans. The *élan* of the National-Socialist movement carried it farther to its highest achievement—the capture of the Congress of Chambers of Commerce, which even under the Republic had had the right of representing the industry of any district with the government, and had statutory rights. On June 22 Dr. von Renteln was elected its president. At this moment even big industry seemed to be bowing its head before the onslaught of the "little man" and to be ready to accept the leadership of the lower middle-classes. Working in the same direction as Wagener amongst the big industrialists, Renteln's aim was the establishment of the Corporate State, with its stable guarantee for all existing classes. The two Corporations he had set up were beginnings. He now promised the establishment of the Corporate State on the basis of the Chambers of Commerce, under the leadership of the lower middle-class.

Economically the situation of the small traders did not progress in the same way. The various measures taken by the government to protect agricultural products injured the small trader particularly, for foodstuffs, eggs, butter, margarine, etc., increased in price, and trade fell. Their chief achievement was the Law for the Protection of Retail Trade of May 12. By this law it was forbidden to open any further retail stores. Expansion of stores was forbidden except to a very small extent, especially the expansion of retail food shops. Sharp punishment was threatened retailers who sold to the injury of other shops or at "usurious" prices. But these concessions to the small traders were accompanied by the prohibition of the erection of independent stalls and artisans' businesses on the premises of the big stores; for this had been the dream of the "little men," to take over stalls in dismantled big stores.

The small traders and artisans awaited in vain, too, for the dismantling of the Consumers' Co-operatives, against which polemic had long been violent.

But the Fighting League had already gone too far. The first signs of the storm gathering over the heads of Renteln's group was the pronouncement of Hitler in the middle of June that there would be no "second revolution". The revolution was now accomplished, said Hitler, and all further change would be evolutionary, legal, and initiated from the top. On June 13 fell the first blow in the economic field. All organisations were forbidden to establish minimum prices for retail goods without governmental sanction. On July 15 the most crushing blow fell, of incalculable importance to the whole of the lower middle-class—the law on Compulsory Cartellisation. This law, instead of realising the inmost desire of the lower classes, the disbanding of trusts and cartels, made cartellisation compulsory if the government so wished it.

The interests of big industry were carrying the day, big industry was organising itself more ruthlessly than ever against the little man. Its counter-attack was successfully entrenched on August 7, when Ley, as leader of the Party Organisation, disbanded the Fighting League of the Middle-Class, and Hess on the same day issued an order that industry must not be tampered with. Later it was announced that only two Corporations existed in Germany—the Corporation of Agriculture and Culture, the creations of Darré and Goebbels respectively. Renteln's attempt at securing a pivotal position for the middle-class in the Corporate State was thus made completely abortive.[1]

This retreat from radicalism, and particularly the continued toleration of the big stores, needed justification. The masses were still in a ferment, and many groups of the Storm Troops were dissolved for their revolutionary zeal. The justification was found in the grandiloquent onslaught on Unemployment launched in the Summer. In terms reminiscent of the excuses of Social-Democracy after 1918, the National-Socialist leaders proclaimed that "German" socialism meant work for all, and that all "experimental" reforms must be put off till later. Existing economic forms were to be strengthened, not weakened. Prices of retail goods were tending to rise, while wages were stable or falling, and nothing should be done to make sales diminish further. The big stores sold at prices most suitable for the masses; their collapse would mean higher prices, increased unemployment, and a considerable loss to their creditors the banks. Thus a stop was put to the disruption of the Big Stores. This was justified on August 5 by the vice-president of the National Corporation of Trade (as it was then called; after Von Renteln's defeat it took the name of National Association of Trade) who stated at the Stuttgart demonstration of the Fighting League that "the government had no intention of changing a single point of the Programme of the National-Socialist Party. Only one thing must be considered, that

[1] A Party Decree of January 11, 1934, goes so far as to forbid all Party members to discuss any future reform of the State.

even institutions which were economically wrong could not and should not be summarily smashed, as no mean portion of public wealth was locked up in them." A month later Ley said similarly, with regard to the Co-operatives, that the penetration of the Co-operatives by independent retailers should take place bit by bit, not too hastily ; "for the time being", no change is to be introduced in the credit and purchasing organisations of the Co-operatives. It is no wonder that at the same time the Bavarian Chambers of Industry and Commerce protested that as yet there was not sufficient control of the Big Stores and Co-operatives, and that the small traders could not compete with them.

By the law of July 15 the irregular rates of taxation directed specially against Big Stores had been regularised at a rate not exceeding double the tax before the National-Socialist advent to power. This step was calculated to be a permanent brake on the Big Stores, and was well calculated ; but the government showed that it did not wish the bankruptcy of the Big Stores. Much of their capital belonged to the banks, many employees worked in them. And so an official definition of a Big Store was given, which freed many Stores from the tax. A Big Store, said the Ministry for Trade, is a Store where many kinds of goods are sold, *including foodstuffs*. If foodstuffs are not sold, the store is not a Big Store in a legal sense (*Warenhaus*). The Big Stores got rid of their food-departments and of the tax as well. Small provision shops profited, but it was a great blow to the whole body of small shopkeepers. A little compensation was won with regard to the seasonal Sales. A series of regulations were issued restricting Sales to certain days in the year and to certain lines of goods—such, for instance, as depreciate with the change of season. The government, however, did not allow the abolition of Sales, as the small shops wanted.

In order to increase their power of competition the small shops adopted two methods. They made use of the temporary stabilisation following the law of May 12 (which was prolonged till June 30, 1934, and then again till September 30), to push prices up, even to press for minimum prices fixed by law. From that time an energetic struggle has been proceeding between government and retailers on this point. In Munich a number of shopkeepers were put for a day into the Concentration Camp for profiteering. Special measures, including the withdrawal of the trading-permit, were threatened against "usurious" prices. In official statements it was reiterated that no minimum prices must be established in important consumption-goods such as foodstuffs,[1] in strong contrast to the minimum prices and attacks on price-cutting in industry. Esser, the Bavarian Minister for Trade, drew attention to the error of applying the principle of concentration to other than big industry; any increase of price by shopkeepers or craftsmen should be energetically opposed by local authorities.[2] In many places action was taken against shopkeepers on this score,

[1] Cf. Order of Ministry of Trade and Industry, May 16, 1934.
[2] *Frankfurter Zeitung*, May 15, 1934.

and craftsmen and peasants selling on the market were equally hit.

The other method adopted in self-defence was the formation and development of common buying-associations for the retailers. Great difficulties here stood in the way. In contrast to the Big Stores, the demand of retailers could not easily be calculated ; but worse than that, credits were hard of access for such organisations. Their securities were not good, being scattered among many small shops, and the banks were not willing to risk much ; this applied not only to private banks but also to Municipal and other public banks. Further, the buying-associations came into direct conflict with the wholesale trade. These matters were the subject of constant discussion, but in some places the buying-associations managed to struggle along.

Not even here was the German government willing to allow a natural strengthening of the position of small enterprises relative to the large concerns. In April and May 1934 the final political line on the matter was defined, not without counter-formulations by the retailers. The National-Socialist organisation within the retail-trade, the *Hago*, first put forward the governmental line, no doubt under pressure. In a statement this organisation defined three reasons for the preservation of the Big Stores [1] : firstly, the Big Stores must not be dissolved since this would mean unemployment for many employees ; secondly, small retailers should not form buying-associations, as this would be simply a counter-measure to the

[1] *Frankfurter Zeitung*, April 14, 1934.

organisations of the Big Stores, and would not lead to a solution of the problem ; thirdly, on the question of bank-credits, the banks must be penetrated by the " idea " that it is necessary to give especial support to small enterprises—though no method is suggested as to how these small enterprises are to find guarantees or security. These decisions, which represent an abject retreat of the small retailer, caused sharp protests, and a week later the *Hago* had to give further reasons. The National-Socialist State, it said, was the natural and determined representative of the trading middle-class ; its chief aim was to protect the small man against the big. Therefore the measures of self-protection necessary under the liberal state were no longer justified ; in practical language, the buying-associations had no longer any right to exist, and must be replaced by the old system of buying direct from wholesale traders. Following on this, the Association of Retail Traders was brought to issue a manifesto recommending harmonious co-operation between wholesale trade, co-operatives, and retail trade, closing with the peccavi : " retail traders must try to free themselves from selfish habits " ! It is no wonder that the *Frankfurter Zeitung* adds : " When one remembers how hard put to it middle-class circles were to recognise the productivity of the wholesale trade, one can see what a distance has been traversed in coming to so positive an attitude." [1]

[1] *Frankfurter Zeitung*, April 21. A characteristic result of the whole " action " of the small tradesmen has been that the number of branches of the German Woolworth increased during 1933 by 14.

What is left to the small retailers and craftsmen? Their power of resistance to the methods of the Big Stores is scarcely increased in the National-Socialist State. The principle of "healthy competition", abandoned in big industry, is preserved for them. The restrictions on the expansion of shops are so hedged about with provisos that they are not effective. The small traders cannot buy cheaply nor fix prices. Their Association is being given more and more the purely technical task of training apprentices for the work and of controlling the admission of new men to the trade. But even admission to the trade is now made conditional only on what is called a "subjective" qualification—to wit, on the political, technical, and moral reliability of the candidate. All the hopes of the lower middle-class, the breaking of the power of the banks, the abolition of the bondage of interest, the dissolution of large enterprises, have been cheated. To their economic subjection is added a political; they may now only prosecute their trade if they are loyal to the government. This is the glorious result of what has been considered the revolution of the lower middle-class.

It is necessary to emphasise this outcome to the struggle of the lower middle-class. Many writers—and chief among them are many Socialists [1]—have seen in the National-Socialist revolution a revolution of this class, the assertion of the policy and power of this class over all other classes. The opportunity has been taken to refute the historical analysis of Marx, who, in defining the absolute antagonism of

[1] Cf. G. D. H. Cole, H. N. Brailsford, etc.

capital and labour, bourgeoisie and proletariat, neglected, it is said, the possibility of a State of the lower middle-class, whose nationalism would be both capitalistic and socialistic. Much might be written on this subject. But in this book we are confining ourselves to an historical account of the National-Socialist revolution. From the purely historical analysis, however, the following points are cardinal. In the " revolutionary " stage of Hitlerism, much of the *élan* of the attack on the social forms of the Republic was borne by the lower middle-class. Many were the pseudo-socialistic theories engendered in this class as panaceas for its ills ; in particular the vague and unpolitical idea of the Corporate State bore up its hopes. But in the National-Socialist State, the few gains made by the lower middle-class in its turbulence were revoked. All leadership was taken out of its hands. It was the cannon-fodder of subtle and powerful generals. Its violent efforts at liberation only embroiled it more and more deeply in the toils of the powers that rule Germany.

The Working-Class

All the public energies of the National-Socialist movement have been concentrated on the working-class—on smashing the institutions of the workers, and on proving to the workers that these institutions injured their true interests. Numberless have been the congresses of workers, the speeches before workers, broadcast into the factories while the machines were stilled. There has been no end to the flattery of the working-class, with constant conjurations to " honour work and respect the working-man ". In the May Day demonstrations of 1934 Göring marched in the procession alongside the workers. Dr. Ley, the leader of the Labour Front, scurries over the land, visiting countless factories and shaking the employees by the hand. Hitler declares that the whole aim of the National-Socialist Party is to secure the working-man his job. " Work is ennobled by National-Socialism ! " he cries. It is true, the working-man is reluctant to listen. He has to be paid for May Day. He has to be marshalled at the factory to ensure that he will march in the procession. He has to be threatened with punishment if he does not go. Those who refuse to listen to the broadcast speeches of the Party leaders are thrown into Concentration Camps. But the first thing is that they should listen, and in this the National-Socialist Party has been successful. What has the Party to say to the working-man ?

The position of the German working-class was not happy after May 2, 1933, when the last of their institutions, the Trade Unions, had been confiscated by the Nazis. Their Parties had been clubbed into illegality. The most militant among the men had been dismissed from the Factory Councils. They were helpless before any attacks on their wages and conditions of life. The State had robbed them of their political liberties. Their employers could threaten anything, and between them and their employers stood only the Trustees of Labour, themselves predominantly from the middle-class, charged with the final responsibility in all matters concerning wage-rates and working-conditions.[1] It was not much consolation that the new leader of the working-class, the Nazi Ley, reassured them that the State was now their guarantee and bore especial consideration for their interests. The State also guaranteed the employers, strengthened the trusts, created cartels. And it was undeniable that the greater part of the prisoners in the Concentration Camps belonged to the working-class. No wonder the workers were sceptical regarding their new masters.

The National-Socialists represented their victory as the victory of the ideal over selfish interest. They reiterated that what was necessary was a change of mind among all classes of society. In spite of this they realised that highly practical, material steps must be taken if they were to win over the working-class to their side. And the most urgent practical matter for the working-class was the question of Unemployment. In January there were 6 million registered unemployed in Germany, and at least 2 million unregistered.[2] The Nazis calculated that if they could bring these unemployed masses into the productive process once again, they would establish their regime upon rock. Strenuously they threw themselves into what was known as the Labour Battle. Their socialism, they said, would manifest itself as work for

[1] For instance, of five Trustees of Labour appointed on April 5, 1934, one was an economist, another a cashier, another a syndic of Employers' Federations in Saxony, another a manufacturer, the last an admiral. The Trustee for Hessen is a banker, etc. etc.

[2] The Census of June 1933 discovered 800,000 of these unregistered unemployed. But most statisticians agree that the number must approximate to 2 millions.

everyone. Curious that in 1918 and 1919 the Social-Democratic Party had repelled attempts at socialisation by this very slogan of " Socialism is Work " !

The Labour Battle of 1933 is not a simple National-Socialist adventure. It reveals their conception of the State, the structure of their State. We can distinguish three aspects of their action—the aspect which embraces the financing of the Employment schemes, the relation between State and employers ; the aspect which concerns the relation between employed and unemployed workers ; that which concerns the unemployed themselves. We will view these aspects in this order.

On February 22 the Hitler government launched the first of its schemes. One hundred million marks were put at the disposal of landowners for repairs and improvements to their buildings. Then on May Day Hitler announced the scheme of building great motor roads all through Germany (decreed on June 27). The first big plan was the Law for the Reduction of Unemployment of June 1. The *Reich* put at the disposal of public bodies and employers a milliard marks, for repairs and improvements on buildings, for land-settlement, and other public works. Money spent in replacing old equipment with new, etc. was to be free of income-tax. The works were to be carried out as far as possible by unemployed, who were to be paid : (1) The unemployment dole they would have received had they remained out of work ; (2) 25 marks from the State for every four full weeks' work, in the form of coupons, exchangeable for clothes, linen, and household utensils; (3) a warm meal per day from their employer, or the equivalent in cash.[1] The financing of the plan was to be covered in the five budgetary years 1934–8.

This law of June 1 was supplemented on September 21 by further financial measures, the latter being known as the Reinhardt Plan, after the Secretary of State in the Ministry of Finance. By this Plan the State promised a contribution of 500 million marks for repairs and expansion of business premises, in the form of contributions of one-fifth of the whole cost of such works. Further, the interest on all other loans made by the entrepreneur for this purpose would be covered by the State up to 4 per cent, payable over a period of six years. It was officially calculated that these arrangements would mean the expenditure of 2 milliards of marks on these works, and would employ one million men. The work was to be carried out through the Winter. These two laws have often been criticised as being a speculation on the future. Unlike Soviet Russia, there is no planned economy in Germany, and there is not the least guarantee that the State will have the money to cover these schemes in the future. The whole charge on the *Reich* of these two plans, together with the Papen Unemployment Plan of 1932, is:

	1933.	1934.	1935.	1936.	1937.	1938.
Million marks	143	652·5	825·0	759·0	754·0	749·0

The *Frankfurter Zeitung* writes of "the burdening

[1] This method, which is fairly expensive, began to be abandoned very soon in favour of the much cheaper Labour Camps.

of the budgets of the future with the troubles of the present". It is a speculation on a possible lightening of the Crisis, and implies, as the Minister for Finance has stated, a "drastic policy of economy" in the future.

These measures can be summed up as strengthening and encouraging capital to undertake new works. A whole series of other laws belong to this category. First the tax was taken off motor-cars and motor-bicycles—a trade important for war-purposes, too—with the result that German motor production has boomed since that time. The agricultural land-tax was lowered, as also the turnover-tax for agricultural produce. Newly built small houses were freed from income-tax, property-tax, and land-tax. Employers were released from further charges by the withdrawal of certain types of workers from the Unemployment Insurance. Domestic helps, agricultural, forestry, and fishery workers were taken out of insurance, so that their employers had no longer to pay contributions for them. Rebate on Income-Tax was granted for domestic helps, in order to encourage their employment.

Thus the main lines of the Labour Battle were, to restore capitalism, to free it from the social shackles which had fettered it. With the employed workers, the mass of the population, it was different. Apart from the continual street-collections in localities, a special Unemployment Subscription was decreed in June. Voluntary in name, it was so only for those who did not draw salaries or wages. Every worker had it subtracted from his weekly wage. Equally, all workers suffered from the short-time worked as a consequence of absorption of additional labour into industry. But three types of workers suffered more particularly the brunt of the Nazi Unemployment policy. In June a first step towards removing women from employment was taken by the so-called Marriage Loan. A loan up to 1,000 marks, to be redeemed 1 per cent per month, was granted to women who had been in work during the preceding six months and who wished to get married. The women had to guarantee that they would not accept further employment so long as their husband's income did not fall lower than 125 marks a month. To provide the money a tax was levied on all unmarried men, subtracted direct from their wage. Politically unreliable workers were excluded from the loan.[1] Together with this a general campaign was begun to get rid of women out of all posts which could be occupied by men. Some Nazi leaders even tried to forbid them from forming National-Socialist Factory Cells. Women, it was said, should mind the home and the children, and were not fitted for responsible work. Only the low wages paid to women-workers (roughly five-eighths of men's rates) rescues them from complete unemployment.

The second class of workers to be hit by the Nazi plan is the young workers. Like the attack on

[1] Striking evidence of the present condition of the working-class is given in the law of March 28, 1934, renewing the marriage-loan decree. Here the figure of the husband's wage of 125 marks (£6) per month, is dropped. The condition for the re-entry of the woman into employment now is that the husband shall be " in necessitous circumstances " according to Poor Law !

employed women, the process of throwing workers under 25 years out of work is still going on. The general form it takes is to force the young worker to go into the Labour Camps, and to make it a condition of employment that he has been for some time in a Labour Camp. Refusal to go into the Camps is rewarded by dismissal, and by the withdrawal of Unemployment Insurance from the young worker. Hierl, the Secretary of State, declared that every person would have to possess a Labour Passport, proving that he had worked in the Labour Camps, before he could enter any trade. No doubt this measure is calculated to serve military purposes as well as to relieve unemployment, for in the Camps the young worker receives military training. But it is also part of a general plan for relieving unemployment. It is characteristic that the 1934 " Göring Plan " for relieving unemployment in Berlin has, as two of its five points, the " replacement of female labour by male, where the work is unsuitable for women ", and the " transference of young workers into agricultural and domestic work ", i.e. into the worst-paid work, which has no Unemployment Insurance.

The third class of workers to bear the burden of the Nazi Unemployment strategy are those who work on the land in the Summer, and normally find employment in the Winter in the towns. These first lost their Unemployment Insurance as land-workers. Then, when in 1934 they attempted to go into the towns to find employment, they were forbidden to do so. First several provincial governments, then finally the *Reich*, in the law to regulate the Migration of Labour (May 15), forbade agricultural workers to enter industrial districts where unemployment existed. Land-workers who leave their parish with the intention of finding work in industrial districts forfeit all right to support from the parish. And employers are entitled to dismiss all men in their employment who have been, during the last three years, employed in agriculture. These workers then, together with young workers and women, find their freedom of choice of occupation, together with their hopes of a decent standard of living, destroyed by the Nazi Unemployment Programme.

The naked skeleton of National-Socialism is seen most clearly, however, in the methods adopted towards the unemployed themselves. From May 1933 to May 1934 it is claimed that registered unemployment dropped from 5 millions to 2½ millions in Germany. If we take those figures at their face-value, they represent a remarkable achievement. Even in England, where production and trade have recovered to an extent far beyond that in Germany, unemployment has only dropped by a million at the outside. What do these figures represent, what methods have been adopted to produce this result?

Apart from the natural method of absorption into the productive process, which can take place only with a revival of production, there are three main methods by which men were taken off the Labour Exchanges and out of the Unemployment figures. These are the Labour Service, organised in Labour

Camps; the Land Helpers; and the Task Work schemes. The Labour Camps originated in voluntary Labour Service schemes, organised often by members of the middle-class, students, etc., where middle-class and workers worked side by side for their keep. They have developed widely since Von Papen's government into Compulsory Camps. All unmarried unemployed, especially those under 25, are forced to enter the Camps on the threat of the withdrawal of their dole. Students are likewise forced to spend at least six months in the Labour Camps, as a pre-condition of studying. In the Labour Camps uniforms are provided, with food and lodging (in barracks usually). The men receive about 1*s.* 6*d.* per week as wage. The work consists usually of amelioration of land, preparing land for settlement, draining, making roads. In many cases friction arise between private firms and the Labour Camps, as it was said that this cheap labour was doing work which should be done by firms paying regular wages to its own workmen. The number of men employed in these Camps has been, since about October 1932, between 200,000 and 300,000. Work is usually about six hours a day, and two or three hours are spent on gymnastics and military evolutions, such as building bridges, digging trenches, etc. Everything is done to command, and the strictest discipline prevails. Political discussions are of course taboo.

Land Helpers are single unemployed or small groups of unemployed who are sent out to work for farmers. They are allotted mainly to the bigger estates, as the smaller farmers and peasantry cannot fill any extra mouths. They receive food and a little pocket-money, and are subject to their employer. It is calculated that there are about 250,000 of them.[1] These men are having particular difficulty in getting back to industrial employment, with its higher standard of living. The law prohibiting agricultural labourers from finding employment in the towns seems to have been made for them.

The third category is the Task Work, very similar to the British schemes. While the work is similar in nature to that done in the Labour Camps—land-amelioration, drainage, etc.—the conditions are different. The work is located not too far from the homes of the workers, so that, while they are usually barracked during the week, they return home for the week-end. As a consequence mainly married men work on the Task-Work schemes. The work is done for private employers or public bodies—landowners, etc.—and the men are paid a wage. Usually the wage is about half the normal rate for similar work ; men receive about 4*d.* to 6*d.* an hour. From their employer they receive also a warm meal per day, or the equivalent in cash. About 600,000 men were employed in Task Work in the Spring of 1934, but even this poorly paid work is too expensive, and in May 100,000 were dismissed. The Labour Camps are, after all, cheaper.[2]

[1] Official statements give their number as 158,000 in January 1934, a month when need of them on the land is lowest.

[2] These figures are taken for the most part from the official publication *Wirtschaft und Statistik*, or from the publications of the *Institut für Konjunkturforschung.*

If we add up the figures of men engaged in Labour Camps, as Land Helpers, in Task Work, reckoning in also political prisoners in Concentration Camps and political refugees (at a moderate estimate, something over 100,000), we arrive at a figure near one and a quarter million. These men are not reckoned in the Unemployment estimates. But even this figure needs correction. In August 1929 the total of employed and unemployed workers (the figures are based on the official Health Insurance returns for the employed, and for the unemployed on the returns of the Unemployment Insurance) was 20,400,005. The combined total in May 1934 was 18,089,460. Two million and a quarter workers have disappeared since the end of 1931 from the statistics! We can assume that most of these are not employed, though some, as always at a time of Crisis, have retired prematurely on Old Age Pensions.

Hitler has, then, by no means solved Unemployment; but the structural aspect of this type of "solution" of Unemployment is important. We have seen that the wages of the men engaged in these schemes are little more than pocket-money. It is difficult to conceive how the families of married men exist on the Task Work wage. But lowness of wage is only a symptom of the whole method. The men are forced to accept this work. They are forced into the Camps, forced to submit to Camp discipline. They have no means of resisting. Strikes have actually occurred—for instance in the Task Work on the Elster River in Köstritz near Gera—but they often result in the abandoning of the work, the workers being then deprived of any support. Not even protests are allowed, there are no organs of self-government. There is no freedom of movement, no choice of occupation possible. Wages are mostly paid in kind—food and clothing—and thus the worker is robbed of one of the most essential conditions of independence, money. The military discipline of the Camps only accentuates this lack of freedom. Only one word characterises these conditions—serfdom. The existence of the German unemployed is a serf-existence. This is the fundamental principle of the Nazi unemployment policy.

To carry through such an enslavement policy energetic methods are necessary in two directions: first, in crushing any criticism or opposition; second, a frontal propagandist attack, to distract attention from the fundamental elements of the policy. As an example we can take the campaign to free East Prussia from unemployment in the Summer and Autumn of 1933. No one who was in Germany at that time was untouched by the barrage of propaganda. All the newspapers bore headlines on the progress of the Labour Battle. The radio brayed constantly with figures and exhortations. As each little district, each parish, got rid of its unemployed telegrams were sent to President Hindenburg or Hitler announcing the glad news. Vivid descriptions were sent from special correspondents. It was a national upheaval, conducted like a war.

What were the facts of the case? The government could not have chosen a more propitious time or a more suitable district for its campaign. East Prussia, a predominantly agricultural area, is particularly subject to seasonal fluctuations in employment, and habitually finds work for 60,000 unemployed in the harvesting months. Formerly Poles had migrated for the Summer into the area, and this was forbidden in 1933. But instead of the unemployed being slowly absorbed during the Summer, the National-Socialists, starting their campaign at the right moment, succeeded in giving these 60,000 work in a week. A great propagandist and organisational coup! Now, however, the real problem remained. There was a surplus of 25,000 agricultural labourers, still unemployed, and, beyond that, between twenty and thirty thousand industrial unemployed, centred mainly in the two towns of Königsberg and Elbing. Efforts were made, by exhortation, to get these industrial workers taken into industry, offices, shops, etc. The result was fair in Königsberg, where 3,000 found temporary work, but in Elbing only 200 were absorbed.

Labour Camps and Task Work centres were established as the only way out; 388 were formed, containing ten to twelve thousand men. The men worked 9 hours per day, married men received 40 pf. (5*d.*) per hour, single men 36 pf. (4*d.*)—i.e. a weekly wage of 16*s.* to 18*s.* The employer gave the men a midday meal, or 3 marks extra per week in lieu thereof. The men under 25 years of age were taken into the Labour Camps, at practically no wage bar their keep, and many men were employed as land helpers. Thus was the Labour Battle of East Prussia won. But nothing had changed in the structure of the economy, and though the Reinhardt Plan provided capital for further work during the Winter unemployment again rose as soon as the harvest was in.[1] In particular, no solution was arrived at for the industrial unemployed of the province, the fundamental problem for the *Reich*. Koch, the President of the province, suggested later a plan for prohibiting the import into East Prussia of goods manufactured elsewhere in Germany, and for industrialising the province to absorb its own unemployed. It is needless to say this plan will not be carried out. It is remarkable that such a plan for internecine economic warfare should have originated in a National-Socialist provincial government !

One more plan of relieving unemployment should be mentioned, as it played a large part in National-Socialist agitation before 1933. This was the plan of land-settlement. The industrial unemployed were to be provided with smallholdings sufficient to hold body and soul together. They would thus be made more or less independent of the market, would become owners instead of proletariat. Land-settlement had gone on steadily since the foundation of the Republic. In general, Task Work prepared the land, draining it, etc., and it was then converted into smallholdings. In 1930, 1931 and 1932 the number of smallholdings formed in this way was 7,441, 9,082 and 9,046 respectively. The National-Socialists

[1] This account of the Labour Battle in East Prussia is taken largely from the *Frankfurter Zeitung* of September 19 and 20, 1933.

had been scornful of these figures. Strasser in the Immediate Programme of 1932 promised smallholdings within one year to 400,000 settlers. Many methods were suggested. The State would lend the settler 40 per cent of the cost and employ the settler on the preparation of the smallholding at Trade-Union rates; the big estates would let some of their land go. What actually did happen? The Hitler government remitted some of the tax off newly erected houses. It appealed to the big estates to give some of their land for the creation of smallholdings. The results were pitiful. The number of smallholdings allotted in 1933 was 4,571, half that in the preceding years; the amount of land little more than half that in 1932. At the same time the principle is observed of increasing the percentage of bigger holdings over 40 acres so that the class of conservative big peasants is strengthened. The land-settlement policy does not make any noticeable difference to the problem of unemployment, and will scarcely cope with the needs of the peasants rendered destitute by the Hereditary Estate Law, who are, according to official statements, to have first claim on the holdings.

The struggle against unemployment stood in the forefront of Nazi activity in 1933 as an end in itself. The methods the government adopted were characteristic. We shall now see how their organisation of the employed workers, of manual labourers and clerks in the factories and offices, reveals the same principles.

Through the general taxation and spending-policy

of Hitler's government, the Crisis in Germany has seemed to grow lighter in the course of 1933 and 1934. Bankruptcies have become more rare. Production has increased—especially in heavy industry, where the production of iron and steel (useful for military purposes) has jumped from 400,000 and 650,000 tons respectively in May 1933 to 700,000 and 1,000,000 in June 1934. An enormous development has taken place in the motor industry, due largely to the new taxation-policy of the government. In January 1933 the number of private motor-cars produced was 2,851, in May 1934, 15,960; commercial cars jumped from 790 to 2,056, motor-bicycles from 2,100 to 10,536 in the same period. The State revenue from taxes was 3 per cent (200 million marks) higher in 1933 than 1932. Wholesale and retail prices rose. But the power of consumption of the masses rose little, and very slowly. The revenue from the taxes levied on articles of general consumption decreased; between April 1933 and March 1934 the revenue from the tax on tobacco dropped by 2·5 per cent, that on sugar by 2·3 per cent, that on beer by 7·2 per cent. Further evidence of the fall in the consumption-power of the working-classes is given by the fact that the revenue from income-tax levied on working-men's wages over 100 marks (£5) per month dropped by 2·5 per cent in this period.

The following figures give a remarkable picture of the impoverishment of the working-class. According to the *Institut für Konjunkturforschung*, the quarterly income of all workers (including clerks and officials) was, in the third quarter of 1933, 6·83 milliard marks; in the fourth quarter, 6·77; in the first quarter of 1934, 6·80. During this period the number of workers employed rose from an average of 13·6 millions in the first period mentioned, to 13·86 in the second period, to 14·351 in the last. The average wage per man per month dropped, as a consequence, from 500 marks in the third quarter of 1933 to 493 marks in the last quarter of 1933, and then to 476 marks in the first quarter of 1934. This would be equivalent to a wage-cut of 5 per cent. Thus we can see, that so far as unemployment was being overcome, it was at the expense of the employed workers.

The smashing of the workers' organisations, industrial and political, was the pre-condition of this policy. Defence was made impossible. The workers were not allowed to have a voice in their affairs. Not even the Corporate State could here be thought of, for in this theoretical social form workers are allowed to discuss and advise. Thus Ley proclaimed: "We are creating not the Corporate State but the National-Socialist State."

The Trade Unions had been broken and absorbed into the Labour Front. This body, however, took over none of the legislative functions of the Trade Unions. It took the Trade Union subscriptions and carries out such functions as insurance, technical classes, etc. It exists to train the workers in National-Socialist ways of thought. It does not allow discussions, there are no Branch meetings, its funds and their disposal are not open to examination. All classes of society belong to it, employers, tradesmen, artisans, as well as the working-class. Its chief creation has been the organisation Strength Through Joy, which aims at controlling the workers' leisure hours, their holidays. The ill-fated ship *Dresden*, which foundered and sank in the North Sea, was chartered by the Strength Through Joy. It makes centres in the towns where the workers may meet of an evening and hear concerts, see films, play billiards. But the workers may not form any clubs of their own, not even to study nature, not even to buy legally published books of their own choosing. The worker may not even leave the Labour Front without running the gravest risk of losing his job. Ley, the leader of the Labour Front, considers the first task to be to win over the workers by meeting them personally and shaking them by the hand. As he said at the Second Labour Congress in May, "I have given my hand to 70,000 working-men; I had nothing else to give them." The Labour Front provides statistics concerning the workers. On the basis of an investigation made in February 1934, it established that the wages of employed German workmen were the lowest in fifty years, an average of 26·22 marks per week [1]—without reckoning contributions and (compulsory) subscriptions mounting in many cases to 9 or 10 marks per week.

The other industrial organisation of the workers, the Factory Councils, were doomed to as radical a transformation as the Trade Unions. They had

[1] The figures do not embrace workers in agriculture, domestic service, and home-industries, the worst paid types of work.

been emasculated in February and March 1933.[1] All matters concerning wage-rates and conditions had been consigned to the care of the Trustee of Labour. From that time they ceased to have any practical importance. In January 1934 the much heralded new Labour Code was decreed. The Trustees of Labour, who had been instituted in the former year provisionally, " until the establishment of the new social order ", were now made permanent functionaries. These National-Socialist officials were made the last instance in all matters affecting working conditions ; they became the immediate dictators of the workers. But a more democratic appearance had to be put on this institution to prevent a too obvious incentive to class-consciousness among the workers. In place of the Factory Councils, Councils of Trust were established. These were to be elected by the workers in the factories. They are formed in the following way. The employer together with the leader of the Nazi factory cell draws up a list of men whom he considers suitable for the post of representatives of the men. The employees are then allowed to elect which of these representatives they wish. Naturally all the representatives are either National-Socialists or " thoroughly reliable " from the point of view of the employer.

The Nazis do not need to explain that this type of election is different from any democratic type. Such a type of representation is a bitter farce. The first

[1] Was it a result of this that the number of accidents in Blast Furnaces and Rolling Mills was 33·66 per cent higher in 1933 than in 1932 ?

elections to these Councils of Trust were held in April. After a short preliminary announcement in the newspapers that all the workers were voting, and 95 per cent for the Nazi candidates, very few detailed reports were given. The reasons seem to have been that the workers were either refusing to vote or were voting for the last candidates on the lists, instead of for the official choices. It was reported in the official Press that at the Leuna works, where there are 12,000 workmen, 800 voted " No ", 900 did not vote, and 2,500 crossed out the whole list. Other reports from all sides indicate that in many factories the National-Socialist candidates were poorly supported, and that millions of workers refused to take part in the elections. This in spite of the fact that refusal to vote was a provocatory act. The elections to the Councils of Trust are a signal that the National-Socialist Party has so far failed in its dearest hope—the winning of the proletariat. Resistance is still largely unorganised, but does express itself if only negatively. The Labour Code is recognised as having deprived the workers of such rights as they had. In their May Day speeches neither Hitler nor any of his staff of speakers mentioned the Labour Code.

In his speech broadcast on August 13 Goebbels mocked the " foreign journalists " who doubt the unity of German people: every workman knows better, he cried. And in the *Reichstag* elections of November 1933, on the question of Germany's withdrawal from the League of Nations, 40 millions of Germans voted for Hitler, against 3 millions only.

But what did these votes mean? To some extent the votes were manipulated. One of the election officials, a former Steel Helmet man, has recounted to the author how, when he reported the figures of his district to the central authorities, they refused to accept his figures, but made him endorse spurious ones, much more favourable to the government. Apart from that, there is a real and substantial fear of severe punishment for Oppositional voters. The case was published of a man who made "improper" remarks on his ballot-paper, who was sought out by the police and punished for it. And punishment takes the forms of personal injury, imprisonment, and dismissal from work and public support. In country districts there has always, even under the Republic, been a control of the voting, particularly in Prussia. The results of elections in Fascist lands give practically no indication of the feeling of the public.

The actual realities are shown in the social structure of Germany. The workers have no rights, no liberties. They are now "followers", their employers are "leaders". They are to learn to obey. If they criticise the leadership, whether economic or political, they are sent to prison and deprived of all means of living. They are to devote themselves to the abstract entity, the German People. Their children learn in the Hitler Youth to obey. But can this system of repression seem to them the metaphysical reality Rosenberg would claim it is? Their whole experience shows it as a political form in which Capital has declared open war on the working-class.

Here, more sharply than under the democratic Republic, the antagonism of Capital and Labour is revealed.

Day after day the German newspapers report the discovery of new Communist activities. Books have been published describing the methods and activity of the Communists.[1] Men just out of Concentration Camps have been given sharp punishments for entering again on their illegal task of building up the resistance of the working-class to the National-Socialist regime. The National-Socialist leaders answer with fiercer and more draconic repression. Göring excels himself in his threats. Nearly a hundred Communists have been beheaded for the deaths of Nazis. The whole country is full of " carpers and grousers ", for where there is no liberty for the workers there is no liberty for any but the small ruling class. No one may criticise, said Goebbels on June 24, but the National-Socialist Party ; and in the Party itself, only those leaders who enjoy the confidence of Industry may speak their mind.[2] These are not assumptions but obvious realities. They are seen by Mr. Baldwin, the Leader of the British Conservative Party, who, in a speech on June 16, said with reference to the British Fascists : " The policy of Fascism is . . . an Ultramontane Conservatism. . . . Communists are drawn in the main from the very poor. Fascists are not, and the

[1] Cf. Martin Sommerfeldt, *Kommune*, March 1934. The author was a high official in Göring's Ministry.

[2] Others are summarily shot, as on June 30, 1934, when 70 Nazi leaders were executed.

idea that the very poor are being singled out for being hit on the head creates a spirit that may be dangerous." In Germany the big interests hold sway. The poor, the working-class, the lower middle-class, have been hit on the head. But they are recovering from their concussion and are already struggling to rise.

CHAPTER X

THE ORGANISATION OF SOCIAL LIFE

In the last chapter the skeleton of the National-Socialist State has been laid bare. Only if we understand this bone-structure can we judge present-day Germany. All Nazi slogans, " nation ", " education ", " law ", " freedom ", " idealism ", etc., can be understood only if we understand the fundamental social facts to which they refer. These facts are : internally, the open oppression of the working-class and the lower middle-class, the prohibition of any political or professional organisations of these classes ; externally, Imperialism taken to its extreme, military and economic warfare against Germany's national rivals. Only in reference to these facts can we understand the " social reforms " of Hitler-Germany, whether they are acclaimed as socialism (the agricultural reforms) or as economic realism (the formation of cartels). Only these facts give us the clue to Germany's statements of foreign policy, its withdrawal from the League of Nations, its pacts with neighbouring countries. Open in his scorn of truth, in his praise of demagogy, Hitler invites us to be critical, to refuse to take his declarations at their face value, to seek for their origins in the general line of his politics.

Fundamental as are the laws of economics of a

society, no society is a mere machine of production and consumption. The mode of production forms the framework, within which men construct those moral laws which are to define the relationships between the members of the various classes. Intellects and feelings have to be formed to affirm the society, to harmonise the classes. As much as the technician has to be trained to create the tools of production, so also the goodwill of the members of the classes has to be won over, so that they devote themselves to the whole. No society simply assumes that men will accept it as it is. Each one creates a system of belief and a general atmosphere of thought, a system of education, which will best weld the members of all classes to the community in which they are born.

There comes a time in all societies when the unity of interest preached by the official philosophy becomes challenged strongly. Thus it is over the whole capitalist world at the present. And such it was most violently in democratic Germany. The Communists challenged not only the economic system of capitalism, but also the whole capitalist system of thought. The National-Socialists saw that, if they were to restore capitalism, they had also to provide a new outlook, with new methods of inculcating their outlook. Communism had grown powerful under democracy. Its logic refuted the arguments of liberalism. The National-Socialists had to remove this challenged liberalism. Their theory of Race was to do this (see Chap. IV). But they had to reorganise the whole cultural and social life of

Germany if their new philosophy was to prevail, if the lower classes were to be won over to a theoretical principle which would reconcile them to the old internal inequalities and strife.

The first step was to destroy any nook where opposition to the regime might lurk. Thus all local powers had to be abolished. The rights of the States, Bavaria, Saxony, etc., even Prussia, were taken from them. Their powers were invested in the central authority of the *Reich* Minister of the Interior, Frick. Hitler's Lieutenants took the place of the old elected governments. Bismarck's work has here been carried to its logical conclusion. By a series of laws the financial competence of the State governments has passed into the hands of the *Reich* Financial Minister. No political Party, except for the National-Socialist Party, exists. No single organisation, whether for politics or for studying nature, whether for professional protection or for singing madrigals, can exist unless it is *gleichgeschaltet*, co-ordinated, provided with Nazi leadership and supervision. An official Censorship may condemn and withdraw books and newspapers which do not contribute to the aims of the National-Socialist Party. The Radio is dominated by the Ministry of Propaganda, which selects the programme and puts the news into the proper form. Goebbels now tells the nation which are the best books of the month—it was a happy coincidence that his latest book was included in the first batch of books recommended to the public. The film is likewise used to ram home the great truths and ideals of the new Germany.

We must examine in some detail the far-reaching changes in the great social organisations, the Law, Education, and the Church.

The Law

The principles of the new Justice of Nazi Germany follow in the main the lines laid down in Rosenberg's *Myth of the Twentieth Century*.[1] The old law and methods of justice were shown to be inadequate in the *Reichstag* Fire trial. At this trial notorious and self-confessed Communists escaped conviction. The methods of the State Prosecutor roused the ridicule and indignation of the whole world. State lawyers were proved to be perjurors, and to use improper methods of examination (*Vogt*). Nazi functionaries contradicted themselves ridiculously, and proved that they had no regard for the truth. The government, in the person of Göring, hurled public threats at one of the accused, Dimitroff, and commanded the High Court to do his bidding. Van der Lubbe, whose physical condition gave cause to grave suspicions, was sentenced according to a law passed after the *Reichstag* had been fired. Dimitroff grew to be a symbol of heroism for the whole world. Evidently this Law and these Courts were inadequate.

The old traditions of Justice, the principles of impartial judges and of individual liberty are thrown on one side. The National-Socialists are forging a Law which shall be a weapon of political warfare, not a system of justice. Before a plenary conference of the Academy of Law, the *Reich* Commissar of

[1] See p. 69.

Justice, Frank, declared (June 26, 1934), that the aim of German Justice is " to serve the People, to change with it, to preserve it ". One of its first aims is to liberate Germany from alien races (the Jews). " It is not a question of formal points of view, but of the substance of the German people ". By " formal points of view " is meant the principle of justice itself. The liveliest acclamation from the distinguished assembly of lawyers and political leaders came when Frank declared : " The creator of this Revolution (the National-Socialist revolution) is at the same time its Lord." The meaning of this became clear four days later, when, on Hitler's own self-confessed responsibility, over 70 Nazi leaders and others were shot without trial. A few days later the Minister for Justice pronounced that this mass execution—the reasons for which have never been explained—was a supremely legal act. When, a month afterwards, Hitler flouted the Constitution and nominated himself President as Hindenburg's successor, the lawyers again approved his act. Yet Frank declares that the Law must rule in Germany. Göring was more honest when he said to a number of leading lawyers : " Only one conception of the Law is valid, and that is the one which the Leader has laid down. You have to act as the Law prescribes and as the government demands of you." [1] Truly the creator of the Nazi Revolution is its Lord ! The *Daily Telegraph* is not too wide of the mark when it describes Hitler as having powers surpassing those of an Oriental despot.

[1] *Berliner Börsen Zeitung*, July 13, 1934.

To correspond to these new principles of justice new Courts of Law have been instituted, the so-called People's Courts. These are to judge charges of treason; and treason by the same decree of May 2 is enlarged to deal with any sort of subversive activity, from the publication of State-secrets to the printing and distribution of illegal pamphlets. There are to be five judges in these Courts, two of whom are lawyers, the others lay judges "chosen for their special experience in combating subversive activities". The panel of these judges, published on July 13, consists of 12 lawyers, 9 officers of the armed forces, 6 high state officials, 5 Nazi Party functionaries. The People's Court is thus a frank instrument of Party vengeance. It reinforces the legal chicanery of Reaction with outspoken National-Socialist principles. Camps have been organised for lawyers, where they will absorb the aims and methods of National-Socialism. No one professing or advocating socialism will escape from these Courts. By August 1934, in the numerous cases of political murder tried since Hitler came to power, in which 92 Anti-Fascists have been condemned to die by the axe, the majority have been condemned only for having "willed" the deed, for having known about it. It is this type of reason which will dominate these People's Courts. The whole function of the Law in Hitler-Germany is the ruthless suppression of Communist, Marxist activities. As clearly as anything else the organisation of this Justice reveals the latent class-war in the land, shows that the National-Socialist State is a form evolved by capitalism to protect itself against the urgent danger from the working-class.

Education

National-Socialist Justice is being fashioned into a sharp instrument of repression, to replace all the irregular methods of Terror which flourished after February 1933. Education, the complement of Justice, is being reformed to inculcate those virtues which Justice maintains by fear. Education is to impress on the mind of youth exclusive loyalty to Hitler and the State. The foreign and internal enemies of Germany and the National-Socialist State are made into objects of loathing. Liberal and socialistic tendencies are rooted out. An ideological barrage of such intensity is created, that the Nazi leaders proudly claim that, when the present generation has died out, the future belongs to them.

The Hitler movement is fundamentally against all modern educational experiments. The child must learn discipline primarily, and the development of the critical faculty is harmful. For Hitler physical instruction takes first place, then the training of feelings and belief, lastly mental education.[1] Thus Montessori and Fröbel establishments have been closed, State grants withdrawn. All secular schools, at which there was no religious instruction, have been closed, many of the teachers finding their way to the Concentration Camps; the National-Socialists insist very strongly on religious instruction. The teacher is to become the Leader of the class, and the system

[1] *Mein Kampf*, pp. 451 ff.

of command is followed. Every year the teachers must join a four-weeks' Camp, where they have a "national-political, scientific, and physical training". Here they will learn how to handle the children according to the new principles.

Jews are of course excluded from teaching in State schools, under the Law for the Restoration of the Official Classes. Jewish children are given a fixed percentage of places in the schools, according to the percentage of Jews in the whole population. But this *numerus clausus* is often disregarded. In Prussia a governmental Order charges schools to give preference to Aryan children. Jews are excluded from Special Schools for mentally defectives. When the classes practise gas-drill, Jewish children are told to go home.

Outside school the children are nearly all organised in the Hitler Youth. Parents have been sentenced to imprisonment for refusing to allow their children to join this auxiliary of the National-Socialist Party. Here they learn Leadership and Discipline. They undertake military exercises, route-marches, crawling on the stomach, etc. When asked about the theoretical training of the Hitler Youth, a small member answered, "We learn map-reading and the morse-code." The children learn to sing the Nazi songs, to take part in mass-demonstrations, to hate the Jews, the French, the Communists.

The position of woman in education corresponds to the position of woman in the National-Socialist State, and is in direct opposition to the practice of Soviet Russia. In industry women are being withdrawn from employment as far as possible. National-Socialist officials went so far as to protest against the formation of Party factory-cells of women. National-Socialist education is to prepare women for motherhood, to make them into willing servants of the men and the nation. "The aim of the education of girls is the coming mother," says Hitler. Care will be given to the training of their feelings, so that they learn to worship the nation and prepare their children for sacrifice to the nation. Their numbers in the teaching profession are to be limited. Men teachers are to be employed increasingly in girls' schools. The proportion of women to men teachers in Training Colleges was in 1933 as 5·3 to 3. This is to be changed in the future to 2 to 3.

In the universities significant steps have been taken towards reorganisation. Here again the principle of centralised political control has been applied. Formerly all the German universities had a certain measure of self-government, though they were State institutions, and were ultimately controlled by the States. But even this small measure of self-government has been taken from them. Formerly the head of the university, the Rector, was elected by the Senate, the professorial body, for one year. Now he is appointed for an indefinite period by the Ministry of Education, and other officials who control the discipline of the students are likewise dependent on the government. Thus direct political control of university life is assured. Jewish professors and university teachers have been dismissed, the report of the Academic Assistance Council of

May 1934 giving the number of ascertained cases as 1,202. Not all these professors have been replaced. For the Nazis aim, for political and economic reasons, at a limitation of the numbers of students. Thus out of a total number of students of 150,000 in 1932, 12,000 were dismissed for political and racial reasons. In the Summer of 1933 the number of students newly matriculating in the universities was 14,000, as against 19,500 in the previous year, a drop of 28 per cent. This is the result of a conscious policy of the government, which does not want so many students. German cultural and economic life can find no room for the young generation, and sees danger in intelligence that cannot be assimilated in the system.

The greatest care is devoted to the political education of the students. In order to study, a favourable testimonial from the school head master is needed, attesting the moral and political fitness of the student. All students must spend at least six months in a Labour Camp, where they are trained in Nazi principles and kept under the eye of Nazi leaders. They must all join the Storm Troops, and carry out the prescribed course of military training. Roughly three nights a week are spent on this training, apart from special duties. Great grumbling has resulted. The authorities at Marburg university, faced with a great fall in the number of students entering for the Winter term, 1934, issued a statement denying the current rumours that the S.A. service at Marburg was exceptionally severe. It was no more severe than elsewhere, they stated, and should not deter students from coming to Marburg. The Storm Troop service is clearly of serious consequences to the students. Work suffers. The same struggle for employment exists now as before Hitler came to power, the same pitiless battle of wits, the same crushing system of examination ; and the poorer German students cannot afford to spend so much time in learning to throw bombs and crawl on their stomachs.

What sort of education is purveyed by this system ? In many ways the curriculum has not changed. Physical training has been developed, but science is still needed. The scientific tasks of the future, the production of synthetic substitutes for raw materials, the development of flying, the automobile and war industries, etc., need a constant flow of highly skilled technicians. Economists are needed. Trained minds of all types are needed in a State which struggles for hegemony in the modern world. But the training, particularly the philosophical training, of young Germany, differs greatly from traditional liberal education. The idea of objective knowledge and science is rejected. The principles of liberal science are, it is stated, rooted in the liberal society. Freedom and objectivity of learning flourished in a society where the State had abdicated and money and privilege ruled. The essential condition of National-Socialist education is the power of the State. This is most marked in those subjects which lend themselves to a selective, biassed treatment, above all in the study of History, where practical politics make their demands most urgently felt.

In most German provinces new guiding lines for the study of History were laid down in the first months of 1933. For that year a special course for schools was decreed, to explain the events of the National Revolution.[1] The starting-point is the War, which is to be represented as an attempt by the whole world to destroy Germany. The War is to be described as an unbroken series of German victories. The breakdown is explained as "the undermining of the German front by alien Marxist spies". Then comes the Revolution of 1918, organised by criminals and murderers; the Treaty of Versailles, bred from the hate of Germany's mortal enemies; the Dawes and Young settlements, the enslavement of Germany. Great emphasis is to be laid on the financial scandals of the Republic, in which Jews were involved, the Barmat, Skarek, affairs, etc. Then comes the national resurgence with Hitler as the noble hero. No mention is made of the social legislation of the Republic, of the rights of the individual it guaranteed.

Frick, the *Reich* Minister of the Interior, promises new History text-books for 1935. Meanwhile guiding lines have been published as follows. Emphasis must be laid on the history of race, on primitive history, as opposed to international history. Social history must be subordinated to political. The idea of leadership, of heroism, must be brought out. The great German heroes, Frederick the Great, Bismarck, are to be adored. The history of Europe

[1] A useful little pamphlet on this matter has been published by the Friends of Europe, called *A Nazi School History Text Book.*

is the work of the Nordic race—the Hindoos, Medes, Persians, Hittites, Greeks are the near kinsmen of the Germans. The fall of these races must be shown to be the result of the bastardising of their blood. Democracy must be shown to be a product of lower, anti-Nordic tribes. And so on through the whole of history. Rosenberg has become the medicine-man of Germany, whose incantations the children must learn off by heart.

This type of history has its offshoots. In the schools great emphasis is now laid on folk-lore and local customs, elementary racial research. In the universities professorial Chairs for Ethnology, or, as it is called, Race-Research, have been founded, and attendance at the lectures of these professors is to some extent compulsory. How expedient a science it is may be judged by the inclusion of the Japanese in the Nordic race, at a time when Hitler's foreign policy made this desirable. A professor of the old school, who refused to make this *volte-face*, was dismissed. An integral part of the new university education is also the establishment of Chairs of military science. The notorious Professor Banse was one of the holders of these new professorships. His books on the new strategy, with his bloodthirsty instructions to young and old to learn all the art of poison-gas warfare and mass-slaughter, were withdrawn only after indignant protests had been made from all over the world.

Is the attempt to eradicate the class-war through education successful? Proletarian children are removed as far as possible from their parents' influence and welded to the State. But the real roots of Communism, the cleft between the classes, are not eradicated through mere friendliness in Hitler Youth and Storm Troops. As the children grow older the stark facts of life loom up darker and darker. The bitter struggle for jobs is no less. Wages drop. Fewer working-class children now can go to the universities—the proportion has dropped more steeply than the general decrease. If in this way working-class children are to be kept from mental training, on the other hand the social antagonism thus engendered will grow.[1]

The political situation in the universities is also serious. The majority of the students were, even before Hitler came to power, in the Nazi student organisation, many in the Storm Troops. Since the cleansing of undesirable elements these Nazi students are in an even higher percentage. But on the whole

[1] The following personal experience of the author, in September 1933, tells its own tale. Two children of well-to-do parents were taken from their Montessori school with its "harmful influence" when the school was closed, and sent to the State school. A day or two later they came home and sang to the parents the following rhymes, which they said all the children sang :

Eins, zwei, drei, Der Hitler legt ein Ei, Die Kommunisten brüten's aus, Und du bist aus.	One, two, three, Hitler lays an egg, The Communists brood it out, And you are out.
Heil, heil, heil ! Der Hitler hängt am Seil, Er wackelt hin und her, O dass es doch kein Hitler wär !	Hail, hail, hail ! Hitler hangs on the rope, He dangles to and fro, O that there were no Hitler !

The parents were horrified at this High Treason !

they represented the more radical wing of National-Socialism. They read the *Tat.* They argued with Socialist and Communist students, and claimed that through the national movement Socialism would come. They expressed the greatest scorn for the bourgeoisie, for its cultural and economic system. Even after Hitler's victory, at international conferences they defended Hitlerism as a socialistic movement, attempting to define a German economy which would correspond to socialistic notions. The consequence was that the leaders of the student organisations had to express this desire for socialism. At a conference of the Students' Labour Service in July 1933 the general criticism was made that Storm Troopers were passed over and former army officers put in charge of the Labour Camps. The increasing militarisation of the Storm Troops, whose political function was taken from them after June 1933, found much dissatisfaction in these circles. The result has been a continual change of leadership. In September Gerhard Krüger was dismissed from his leadership of the *Deutsche Studentenschaft*, after writing an article on " Our Obligation to Socialism ". In July 1934 all the leading officials of the Students' League were dismissed, and a thorough investigation of the student question announced by the Party leaders. The vexed question of the aristocratic Corps students remains unsettled. The Nazi students, during the June campaign " Against Carpers ", had attacked the Corps students in several universities. The Party authorities, while using bland words, had taken the Corps students under their protection. Even the little world of the students mirrors truly the general political situation. Here also Reaction is reaping where the " revolutionaries " sowed. And, equally inevitably, the Opposition is forming against the Reaction and against the National-Socialist Party which has given it a new lease of life.

The Lutheran Church

Much more than education, the Christian Churches claim to base themselves on absolute principles, which neither time nor expediency can undermine. How were they in Germany to direct themselves into new paths, to condone slaughter and fire-breathing, to accept the worship of Race? We need not concern ourselves with those small communities which taught pacifism or community of goods, which were placed under State supervision or broken up. We will deal first with the Lutheran Church, the State-Church, and then with the Universal Church of Rome.

Lutheranism was for Hitler, it would seem, the very tool he could wish for. The Head of the State is the Head of this Church. He can control dogma and religious observance. With the idea of individual salvation the Lutheran Church combines absolute subservience to the Powers that be in the secular sphere. It denies to the subject all political rights. When Gospel and State come into conflict, the State must be given the preference on this earth. If the rulers of the world err, only God has the prerogative of punishing them. Thus this Church could not offer opposition to Hitler. But the Lutheran Church had also serious drawbacks. Distinguished ecclesiastical historians such as Troeltsch have remarked that the Lutheran Church is estranged from the working-class, and that this estrangement is due to political antagonism, not dogmatic. Nobility and upper middle-class belonged to it, but not the masses. At the same time there had grown up within this Church, since the eighteenth century, types of theologians who largely disregarded the dogma of Luther and Melanchthon, and reinterpreted Christ's doctrine in terms of their own philosophy. This freedom they arrogated led them into paths of liberalism, even of religious socialism. Thus the Nazis could not be satisfied to give the Church a new secular head. They had to cauterise dangerous tendencies, and to attempt to infuse new vigour into this living corpse by giving it contact with the masses.

The Nazis set themselves a threefold task, as complex as their whole political action. They had to attack the ultra-conservatives of the Church, who, like the German Nationalists, did not realise that the times needed new forms, and that the masses could not simply be ignored. They had to attack those clergy who wished to preserve liberal democratic traditions, the right for the individual to think and believe as he thought best. They had to formulate a religion which would appeal to the masses.

Their first step was the unification of the Lutheran Churches. In place of the manifold State churches, with their own constitutions and privileges, where opposition of the most varied types could flourish, one centralised *Reich* Evangelical Church was founded, with a *Reich* Bishop at its head. The Bishop is elected by the National Synod, and together with a Spiritual Ministry of four controls the whole theology, morals, and politics of the Church, " according to the Gospel of Christ and the Witness of the Reformation ". The Constitution of the Church (July 11, 1933) recognises in its Preamble the National Revolution as a " great turning-point in history ". But, united in the formation of the Constitution, grave differences immediately appeared in the Church. The first Bishop, Dr. von Bodelschwingh, was deposed shortly after his election by Nazi pressure, and a veteran Nazi pastor, Müller, a former chaplain to the Forces, was elected in his place by the simple expedient of forcing the opposition from the election chamber. Further, the Evangelical Youth organisations were absorbed in the Hitler Youth, and thus removed from Church influence. From then till now a sharp struggle has raged, the result of which is still undecided.

The National-Socialist clergy is organised in the movement of the German Christians. The manifesto of this movement demands the abolition of all vestige of democratic election in the Church. A sharper attack on " Mammonism, Bolshevism, Pacifism " is urged. The eternal truth of God is to be delivered in a form comprehensible to the German people. The ultimate principle of religion is " service to our Race "—" We will serve through our Church our God, and for that very reason our

Fatherland ". The spirit of international Christianity must be eradicated by the belief in the " divine mission of the German people ". The mission to the Jews is to disappear, and the Nordic Race must be protected against all harmful elements. Pity, Love, Philanthropy are to disappear, to be replaced by obedience to the Race, the People, the Nation. It is useless to try to establish connexions between the German Christians and Christ's doctrine. They are nationalists of the Rosenberg type, fanatical and ruthless, who wish to utilise the store of belief and credulity in the Christian Church for national ends. God and Christ are merely subsidiary to the nation, give the concept of the People an aureole. It is an attempt to link up the Church with the National-Socialist movement, to provide the Church with a mass following. It may be said here that the majority of Nazis look on at their theologians with cynicism, eager to have control over the clergy, and not worrying overmuch what are the reasons given.

The German Christians carried all before them in the first months of Hitler's power. Their nominee became *Reich* Bishop. Their meetings were enthusiastically attended. But they overstepped the mark. They went farther and farther away from Christianity, ending with the old Germanic cult of Wotan, etc., worshipping the principles of heroism and loyalty. At a great meeting in Berlin their spokesman thundered hatred against Paul, " Rabbi Paul ", the Jewish preacher of Charity. The Church dignitaries on the platform did not object. Roman Catholicism came in for its share of vituperation as an alien religion. Christianity was becoming purely German, purely anti-Socialistic, purely militaristic.

The first opposition came from small circles of theologians in the Summer of 1933. The *Jungreformatorische* movement opposed the exclusion of the Jews from the Church, though affirming the new State and the authoritarian principles of the new Church. Resolute opposition came first from the theologian Karl Barth, with his pamphlet *Theological Existence To-day!* He opposed the thesis that the reforms in the State had anything to do with religion, and set himself against any new Constitution of the Church. Quoting Hitler's promise in his *Reichstag* speech of March 23, 1933, to the effect that the new government would in no way interfere with the rights of the Church or change her relationship to the State, he called for a renewal of religion from the heart. The Church, he says, should carry out her task of preaching the Gospel within the National-Socialist State, as in other States, but not make it her task to preach the gospel *of* the National-Socialist State.

This courageous manifesto was like a beacon of hope to a middle-class which in all other matters had driven helplessly before the Nazi storm. On its principles the Church Opposition was built up, the Pastors' Emergency League, its leader the Berlin pastor, Niemöller, a former submarine commander, its main strength in Berlin and Westphalia.

Very soon the dogmatic arguments had been reduced to arguments of might. Müller tried, by decrees, prohibitions, imprisonment, to assert his will, Niemöller and his group stoutly resisting all attempts at linking the Church irrevocably to the National-Socialist doctrine. The State had pledged itself not to interfere in internal Church affairs. But since the German Christians had won for their movement the Primacy, the State was enlisted on their side. All refusal to do Müller's bidding was a breach of the Church Constitution, and thus punishable by law. As a result many pastors were fined and imprisoned. The usual Nazi tactics were evident in this struggle. On one day Müller would shower blandishments and bribes on the Opposition, on the next he would use violence.

The effects of the struggle within the Church are complex. On the one hand the extreme German Christians have suffered defeat. Their champion, Hossenfelder, has been dismissed from his post as Bishop of Berlin. There is no official support for the bloodthirsty paganism they advocate, though it is not prohibited. On the other hand the Church has remained under Müller's leadership, and this leadership has become absolute and dictatorial. The National Synod, meeting on August 11, 1934, voted away its right of control over the *Reich* Bishop. Two laws were passed, which effected all that Hitler and Rosenberg could desire. Firstly, the passing of laws is in future to be the prerogative of the Spiritual Ministry of Four, the Council which Müller appoints; and secondly, all pastors and Church officials must henceforth swear an oath of allegiance to Hitler.

By these laws the Lutheran religion and the Lutheran Church are bound irrevocably to the State of Hitler. The Opposition of the lower clergy, of the Pastors' Emergency League, is made illegal. Already a frontal attack has taken place, five provincial pastors being convicted of subversive activities and sentenced to imprisonment in June. This precedent will be the basis of future action. Niemöller himself has so far been treated with deference, because of the great popularity he enjoys. No doubt the authorities are biding their time till they can make a sensational disclosure of "treasonable" activities between Niemöller and his friends, so as to swing over popular opinion. Meanwhile, he preaches in his Dahlem church, in spite of bans against him, and attracts big congregations.

For this struggle has not been a theologians' quarrel. As the Opposition grew it attracted more and more people to its churches. It is true, these new Church members were mostly of the middle-class; the working-class is still distant from the Lutheran Church. But the change of outlook which National-Socialism demanded could not be accomplished easily, or by all men who abhorred Communism or Socialism. Even for the middle-class certain precious liberties are lost under Fascism, rights of free thought, free organisation. Cowed and bullied by the arguments and power of National-Socialism on the political and social field, the middle-class sought to rescue some of its old freedom in the religious sphere. All this Opposition clergy protested their acceptance of the State of Hitler, but they wished to keep religion as a cult superior to and different from political belief. The question was, How far could the totalitarian State tolerate individual freedom? The answer has been given. In no degree. No thought which does not positively serve the ends of the National-Socialist State can be permitted. In all freedom lies the germ of subversive political activity. Here again the middle-class, which once flocked to Hitler's banners, has learnt the meaning underlying National-Socialism.

The Roman Catholic Church

Constitution and dogma of the Lutheran Churches made them into suitable instruments of the National-Socialist State. It is otherwise with the Catholic Church. Since Bismarck's attack on the Catholics, the latter have formed in Germany a strong political Party with its own political aims. Though the Party went into liquidation in July 1933, the tradition of political struggle still exists in Catholic ranks. Further, the Catholic Church has a strong mass-basis. It is especially strong among the working-class of the Rhine Lands and Bavaria. And its leadership, the Pope of Rome, is situated outside of Germany, a world-power of some strength, not easily to be domineered by national powers. In the main the Catholics had shown that they agreed to Hitler's advent to power. Brüning had prepared the way for a national dictatorship, had negotiated with Hitler. Relying on very substantial promises from Hitler, the Centre had voted for Hitler's government on March 23, 1933. But within the bounds of this general approval of National-Socialism, organised opposition to Hitler could be expected from the Catholics on matters touching the freedom of the Catholics to pursue their religion, to carry on their social and cultural work. Immediate steps were taken to establish these rights in a Concordat. But negotiations are dragging on lamely. Those agreements which are reached round the council table are nullified repeatedly by political action.

In the Catholic Church there could be no question, of course, of modifications of dogma in favour of Hitlerism. Service to God is the antithesis for it of service to the world, and this is expressed in practice by the antithesis : the conscience belongs to the Pope, the body to Hitler. The whole problem can be expressed in the metaphysical question, What is body and what is soul? What are the relations between the two? Luther broke from the Papacy in his interpretation of this problem. The Papacy now has interpreted it by renouncing political action in Germany. But the kernel of the problem is revealed on the matter of the Catholic social and cultural organisations, especially the Youth Organisation. Does this belong to the soul?—for it is built on a purely confessional basis; or does it belong to the body, to the State?—for it is an organisation of young *people*, not merely of consciences. So the centre of the struggle between Hitler and the Pope is the Catholic Youth Organisation.

The Hitler government has expressly guaranteed the Catholic Youth Organisation. Nevertheless, all subterfuges are adopted to disrupt it and break its power. Its meetings and demonstrations have been dispersed by violence. A Catholic Congress of Youth was broken up and had to be abandoned. Since nearly all young people are brought, by one way or another, into the Hitler Youth, an effective counterblast to Catholic teaching is here prepared. In 1934 more open measures were taken by the National-Socialist authorities. Catholic Youth organisations were forbidden to demonstrate in the streets—even on Holy Days—and to wear distinctive dress or signs, to make holiday excursions and hold holiday camps. Catholic newspapers are subject to confiscation, parish magazines have been prohibited in great numbers for criticising the government's ecclesiastual policy. Even messages from the Pope are kept from the newspapers. The wildest charges of subversive political agitation are made against Church dignitaries, resulting in hostile demonstrations such as that on April 7 outside the palace of the Bishop of Würzburg, when the crowd was incited to hang the leaders of the Catholic Youth, including the Bishop.

For some time the Catholic Church was patient in the face of these attacks, trusting in the Concordat negotiations. But the repeated provocations spurred it to decisive statements. The leadership of the Catholic action was entrusted to the South German, Cardinal Faulhaber. This man is no radical. In the period of the Republic he publicly branded the government as perjurors and traitors. He was of the Ultramontane school, desiring the restoration of the Bavarian monarchy. Yet as early as 1922 he had come into conflict with the National-Socialists, condemning their militarism and murderous agitation. Now this ultra-conservative Roman prelate turned his fury on the religion of the German Christians, on the whole dogma of the Race. In his Advent sermons of 1933, published under the title of "Judaism, Christianity, and Germany", he scourged the Anti-Semitism and Paganism of the Nazi theologians. A bitter battle ensued between Rosenberg and him, and the former's writings were placed on the Index—with other famous writers, as Rosenberg said. Other Catholic prelates entered the lists, such as the Bishop of Berlin, Dr. Bares, who openly attacked Rosenberg's doctrines. The National-Socialist Press answered, led by the *Völkischer Beobachter*, with cynical calumny. When the Duisburg Catholic paper brought a lawsuit against the local National-Socialist paper on the grounds of illegal methods of advertisement—which had consisted in calumniating the Catholic paper—the Duisburg Law Court rejected the charge, stating in its summing up that "the so-called Catholic Press is superfluous" (*Germania*, April 4).

Where the conflict is leading cannot be precisely predicted. Only the general causes can be understood. The Catholics have in the past been opposed to a strong centralised system in Germany. Under the old small State system the Catholic Church enjoyed far greater privileges and powers than at present. Their claim for the independence of the Youth Organisations has been no doubt strengthened by the influx of Communist and Socialist young workers into them. Wherever any liberty is assured, there the Opposition to Hitler will flock. But apart from these internal causes of conflict, probably the causes for the greatest bitterness lie over Germany's frontiers. The regime of Dollfuss was blessed by the Pope. As the Church conflict sharpened in Germany, so the efforts of the Church grew stronger to keep Austria apart from Germany. The Austrian Catholic Party, the Christian Socialists, was the core of the Dollfuss dictatorship. For the Nazis this simply bore out all their theories of the Roman Church. Once again it was clear that Rome was opposed to the unity of the German race.

Further repercussions abroad are felt in the Saar. The Saar has a predominantly Catholic population. Before Hitler came to grips with the Church it seemed certain that this territory would, as a result of the coming plebiscite, be reunited with Germany. Socialist and Communist opposition did not command a majority. But the Nazis have seriously endangered their chances. In some places Catholics are uniting with the radical Parties in the demand for a Saar republic. The situation has been made worse by the lawless assassination of Catholics in Germany, such as the leader of the Catholic Action, Dr. Klausener, and Von Papen's secretary, and the senseless disregarding of Catholic susceptibilities when they were cremated instead of being accorded the due Catholic burial rites. It is difficult to see how Hitler will be able to effect a reconciliation with the Church before the plebiscite in January next.

We cannot foretell the future. We can, however, distinguish the motive forces of history. The main principle for the National-Socialist government is that religion shall serve the State. Hitler has often, both in *Mein Kampf* and during these past months, expressed his aversion from dogmatic squabbles. He writes: "My movement sees in both religious Confessions equally valuable struts to the fabric of our people." And history shows that for the last three centuries Lutheranism and Catholicism have been from the political point of view conservative forces, tending to the preservation of the political *status quo*. No word of political antagonism to Hitler's power has been breathed by the religious leaders since 1933. Why does not the National-Socialist movement satisfy itself with this, and leave theology alone?

This is a social question, not a question of wild fanaticism. Partly, as has been said, no nooks must be left where the Opposition may meet and organise support. But the Nazis have attacked more than the social and cultural organisations of the Churches. This theoretical extremism is a part of the whole extremism of National-Socialism. It is a product of that distress of certain social classes, mainly of the lower middle-class, which demanded, through the Hitler movement, a complete reorganisation of the national life. Like Anti-Semitism, it was not directed against those responsible for this distress, but against powers who were imagined to be effecting Germany's downfall. Since Hitler came to power, as has been shown in Chapter IX, the radicals, the lower middle-class supporters of National-Socialism, have been progressively suppressed. The State has been delivered over to the big interests. But outlets must be preserved for the passions of the radicals. The disillusionment in practical politics must be covered over by the solace of imaginary victories. It was widely foretold in 1933 that the Nazi Anti-Semitism would soon be suppressed, since it served no useful purpose and only harmed the State. But Anti-Semitism has remained, has even taken more efficient forms. The same is true of the religious fanaticism of the German Christians. It serves the necessary function of giving the government the appearance of radicalism, and thus satisfies the unrest of the Nazi " revolutionaries ". When it becomes too harmful for the State—as the events in Austria and the Saar seem to indicate—it will be thrown aside, its leaders cast into obscurity or assassinated. But when that happens, one more group will have been alienated from the National-Socialist State, the lower middle-class will have been brought still closer to the Communists.

CHAPTER XI

THE PRESENT SITUATION

Economic Recovery and Collapse

In this book, for purposes of convenience, the economic Crisis has been discussed as if it were a phenomenon existing between 1929 and 1933. But though Hitler's advent to power put a new face on economic problems, it did not abolish them. Germany is still in the throes of the Crisis. In this she is not alone. England has shown, of all countries, the most marked recovery, though even in England it is admitted to be instable. But in most countries the Crisis is almost as severe as ever. The gigantic scheme of spending entered on by the United States of America, though producing an improvement in some branches of industry, has not established anything like a stable recovery, and has let loose the class-war in all its fury.[1] Production in France, Italy, Switzerland, Holland and Belgium has scarcely moved out of its stagnation. And, above all, where a partial recovery has been effected, in England, U.S.A., Japan, and Germany, this recovery represents in no way a harmonious world-development, but a set of parallel, isolated recoveries, often in desperate rivalry to one

[1] See the valuable booklet, *The Roosevelt Illusion*, by Burns and Roy.

another. Exchange between countries stagnates. There is no world-movement of relief.

The recovery in Germany is representative of this development. The index of production, which rose in 1933 from 62·9 to 75·1 (1928 = 100), reached 86·2 in April 1934. The value of production, 20·6 milliards of marks in the first quarter of 1929, rose from 9·2 milliards to 11·8 milliards in the corresponding period of 1933 and 1934. The amount of production in heavy industry, building, textiles, for the first quarter of 1934 was respectively 65 per cent, 93 per cent, and 26 per cent, higher than in the corresponding period of the previous year. Yet at the same time exports dropped abysmally. The monthly average of exports dropped from 799 million marks in 1931 to 478·3 in 1932, 405·9 in 1933, and 344·5 for the first six months of 1934. Imports, on the other hand, have touched a much higher monthly average in 1934 than in 1933 (384·3 million marks as against 350·3). The consequence is that for the first time since 1928 imports exceed exports. In place of the export surplus of 963·7 millions for the first half-year of 1931, from January to June 1934 there was an import surplus of 216·4 millions.

The recovery of trade in Germany is not, then, based on an increase of the export trade. She has lost even her traditional markets in the Scandinavian countries and Finland. Nor has the home market expanded noticeably. The whole income of the employed classes has increased only slightly. Retail sales show a slight increase only in the second quarter of 1934. On what is this recovery based?

All official and semi-official publications in Germany are united in ascribing the recovery of production to the governmental measures for creating employment.[1] By the Papen, Immediate, and Reinhardt Plans, about 5 milliards of marks were put at the disposal of employers and public bodies, for renewals and improvements, for railway development and for the building of the Motor Roads. This vast scheme for stimulating capitalist enterprise is mainly responsible for the increase in production and its absorption. But everyone in Germany is now asking, what will replace this spending policy? Most of the money is already gone, and constitutes a heavy charge on the budgets of the next five years. No more spending can be thought of. The Finance Minister has several times already proclaimed the devolution of the labour-producing measures, and has demanded severest economies in all departments of State and local government (see his speech of June 13, 1934). The gold reserve of the *Reichsbank* dwindles. Already these ardent and intransigent nationalists are attempting to negotiate loans abroad, in London and America, where, according to the *New York Times*, they have found temporary support on hard terms. Thus they break the bondage of international capital!

Above all the German government looks for a revival of export. This has been a constant theme in the Business Congresses of this year (e.g. that at Hamburg on April 19). Germany no longer has the money to pay for its imports. The method of allow-

[1] See, for instance, *Wirtschaft und Statistik*, No. 14, 1934; and the *Halbjahresbericht der Reichskreditgesellschaft*, July 1934.

ing foreign importers of German goods to pay in "blocked" or "scrip" marks at a 30 or 50 per cent discount does not cope with this problem. The unfavourable balance of trade has led to a general State control and restriction of imports. When a shortage of potatoes occurred in July, no money was available for purchasing from abroad, and queues formed in front of the shops. Export must be developed. The difficulties in the way are great. Germany has no colonies, and therefore must buy its raw materials abroad. The production of synthetic substitutes, which has gone to astonishing lengths, is still, in most cases, too expensive to be profitable. And, owing to the high cost of living, due to the agricultural policy of the government, working expenses are high. The alternatives of inflation and a thorough campaign of wage-cuts present themselves as the only possible solution; or probably both will be applied. Already a modified form of inflation exists in the subsidies (through the blocked and scrip marks) to the export trade. And a first step to a programme of wage-cuts is seen in the decree limiting the hours of work of textile-workers to a maximum of 36 hours per week (July 1934). But the social repercussions of inflation and wage-cuts make them feared. Middle-class would be joined with working-class in opposition to the government.

Another aspect of the recovery of production in Germany must be pointed out. By far the largest part of the profit has gone to the shareholders, in the form of increased dividends, or of strengthened reserves. The *Deutsche Zeitung* reports, that of 93 Joint-Stock Companies examined in the year 1933–4, 81 made a profit and only 12 a loss ; 31 of the former used their profits to cover former losses or to fill up their reserves ; 50 of them were in a position to pay dividends, larger dividends than in the preceding year in all but three cases. The *Völkischer Beobachter* itself is forced to make caustic comments on those firms who utilise the National-Socialist revolution to pay higher dividends. The *Deutsche Zeitung*, the organ of the Agricultural Corporation (*Darré*), asks openly, does not this behaviour openly contradict National-Socialist thought, since the prosperity of industry is due entirely " to the sacrifices of the whole nation, as embodied in the governmental subsidies ? " (July 29). It seems that only the possessing classes are to profit from the " national resurgence ".[1]

Germany's recovery brings her face to face with two main facts. Internally, the unrest and struggle between the classes grows. Abroad, she finds each nation protecting its market against her goods. The world, the *Reich* Credit Society complains, has lost its " economic conscience ". Room should be made for every country in the markets for export. This from National-Socialist Germany ! Needless to say, room will not be made by peaceful means for Germany's trade. And so the ultimate method is left, by which internal and foreign difficulties will be overcome—War. For this eventuality the National-Socialist Party has been preparing itself for 15 years.

[1] It must be remembered that Point 13 of the Party Programme demands that employees of big concerns shall share in the profits.

We have seen how all its social schemes, for unemployed and children, for teachers and lawyers, etc., are built to the needs of war. Concretely, too, Germany is preparing for war. She is the largest importer of nickel from Canada, necessary in the war industries. To this account must go the great development of heavy industry in this past year. Forbidden by Treaty to make military aeroplanes, she buys aeroplane engines from all lands. Recently Sir John Simon in the House of Commons admitted that Armstrong-Siddeley's had sold the German government 90 engines. Germany's military estimates for 1934 reveal where a government in an economic crisis finds it worth while to spend :

	1933.	1934.	Increase.
	in millions of marks.		
Navy . . .	183	233	50
Army . . .	472	647	175
Air . . .	78	210	132

These are the blood and iron basis to a philosophy which exalts war as the noblest expression of the race.

Germany and the Great Powers

The war which Germany wishes to fight is that against Soviet Russia, as expressed in the memorandum presented by the then Minister, Hugenberg, at the World Economic Conference in June 1933. But allies are needed. England above all was to be won over to the German cause. Through her foreign policy Germany has, however, fallen into the most absolute isolation.

Hitler's calculation was that he would win the

goodwill of the capitalist world through his ruthless extermination of Communism, and that this goodwill could be organised to approve a common onslaught on Soviet Russia. Though the terroristic methods used, and especially the persecution of the Jews, alienated sympathy for the time being, this calculation showed itself on the whole correct during 1933 and the early part of 1934. *The Times* changed its attitude from unfriendly to friendly in the Autumn. It opened its columns to very favourable articles—for example those on Hitler's Unemployment policy on January 31, February 1 and 2. Bishops who protested against Hitler's Anti-Semitism were eager to add their recognition of the moral revolution the Nazis had effected. It was seen that Hitler was not going to be "experimental", was not going to tamper with capitalism, nor to throw overboard the old ruling class. True, German finance was considered speculative, and definite opposition was made to the attempt to suspend payments on the Dawes and Young loans. But there seemed to be a real rapprochement between England and Germany.

But Hitler was not able to steer a clear course. Two events led to his (perhaps temporary) isolation, the murder of Dollfuss, coupled with his whole Austrian policy, and the revolt in the Storm Troops.

It was not general Nazi opinion which determined the German policy towards Austria. Nazi opinion has often enough been ignored since Hitler came to power, and the ruling circles of industrialists and bankers would not allow the desire for the unity of the German race to maintain itself against their needs. But big industry itself had a vital interest in Austria. With a united Austro-Germany an advanced post would be cast out towards the Balkans. The proximity of a Great Power to Jugo-Slavia, Hungary, Roumania, and Bulgaria would have good effects on trade.[1] Further, Czecho-Slovakia would be engirt by Germany on three sides, a fact of decided military importance. These economic and military reasons decided the aggressive Nazi campaign against the Austrian government. Nazi legionaries who had left Austria were armed and barracked near the Austrian frontier. The notorious Frauenfeld, the leader of the Nazi Party in Austria, broadcast his virulent propaganda regularly from the Munich wireless station. A special Austrian department of the Nazi Party existed, under Habicht. Arms and explosives were smuggled over the frontier, leading to the demonstrative campaign against Dollfuss, to end with the Austrian Chancellor's assassination.

The Great European Powers were, however, resolutely opposed to Germany's dreams of expansion. Italy, so friendly otherwise to the sister Fascist Power, was obdurate regarding the " independence " of Austria, dreading Germany as a neighbour and rival in Eastern Europe. France would put every possible obstacle in the way of Germany's development. England, too, showed that, whatever other aims she has, she is resolutely against a powerful Germany, who may one day again challenge England's position

[1] See the book of Giselher Wirsing, *Deutschland in der Weltpolitik*, in which the author creates an imaginary economic bloc in Central and Eastern Europe, under the hegemony of Germany.

in the world. Thus the post-War policy of supporting Austria by loans was continued at the crisis caused by the death of Dollfuss. All the three Powers hastened to guarantee Austria's independence, and to protest in Berlin against the Nazi action. Italy even mobilised her troops on the frontier. It was a *débâcle* for Hitler's foreign policy. Not all Goebbels's sardonic wit about the poison of the foreign journalists in Rome, Paris, and London, can cover over the fact of Germany's isolation and weakness.

The effect of the assassination of Dollfuss was all the greater because of the events in Germany at the end of June. Hitler, at the head of his Guards (the S.S.), swooped down on June 30 on the Chief of the Storm Troops, Röhm, and many other Storm Troop leaders. Many were shot without trial. At the same time members of the Nationalist wing were killed. Von Papen was put under arrest and his secretary killed. General Schleicher and his wife were shot. The reasons have never been explained. Hitler accused the dead men of preparing revolt, though against what is not clear ; he justified his action further by referring to the " bestial vices " of Röhm, Heines and their friends. But moral indignation swept over the rest of the world. The reasons are not far to seek. These sudden executions proved that National-Socialism is a lawless government, which may arbitrarily destroy any citizens whom it wishes out of the way. It opens the way for private vendettas and treachery. While it provides a guarantee for capitalism, it removes any rival personalities from the scene by violence. Such a government will be tolerated only by a ruling class which has been shaken to its very foundations by the internal social struggle.

The effects of this "gangsterdom" were most marked in England, the potential ally of Germany. Within the country it led immediately to disclaimers of the Mosley Fascists by Lords Northcliffe and Nuffield. In foreign affairs it contributed to the decisive action at the time of the assassination of Dollfuss, and to the classic declaration of Baldwin that henceforth England's frontiers were the Rhine. It is true that such moral indignation, the fear of such lawlessness, is not a permanent political factor. Even more serious infringement on "rights" and "moral laws" took place when the Japanese attacked China in 1931 and 1932. But for the time being, and in a period when the English government can maintain itself by its laws, Nazi gangsterdom has helped to bring about Germany's political isolation —an isolation which is reflected in the malicious resentment of the recent pronouncements of Nazi leaders.

The Class-War

For many reasons the inner-political situation in Germany is tense. There is the mass-disappointment at the failure of the socialistic programme. The increased power of the possessing class is brought home inexorably to the workers and lower middle-class. The clearest political evidence of the Reaction is to be seen in the history of the Storm Troops.

The S.A. were, in the main, the revolutionary forces of National-Socialism. In their rank and file the socialistic dreams of the Nazis were nurtured. During 1932 they clamoured for the *coup d'état* which Hitler did not wish for, and often threatened to get out of hand. In 1933 they formed the terror-bands who for a short time dominated whole districts. They were apotheosised as the symbol of the Nazi revolution. Books on the S.A. (e.g. by Killinger, Röhm, Hoffmann, etc.) extol the ruthless revolutionary spirit of the Troops, their scorn of all established authority. At the Nürnberg Party Congress in 1933, Hitler was accompanied in the most solemn rite by Röhm, the S.A. Chief-of-Staff, alone. But, in proportion as National-Socialism revealed itself as Reaction, the S.A. had to lose its importance and change its function. It had to become the tool of Reaction, a police-army. And this change could not take place peacefully.

While on the one hand mutterings in the rank and file arose, grumblings about the treachery of the Nazi leaders, the will developed to maintain the S.A. in its old form. The S.A. leaders, threatened with a minor rôle in the new State, struggled for the maintenance of their power. Röhm, elevated to a Ministerial post in 1933, began to scheme for a "second revolution" which would get rid of Hitler's advisers and make of the S.A. the core of a new army. These tendencies were evident from the end of 1933. The government also took its measures. A great campaign "Against Carpers and Grousers" in June 1934 was utilised for a demagogic attack on the "Reaction", though in reality the grousers were the radicals who had hoped for socialism, the lower classes who complained of the prices of foodstuffs, etc. At the same time protective measures against the Storm Troops were taken. The Hitler Guards (S.S.), a body of picked men instituted in 1926 to protect the Leader against his own Storm Troopers, were given important police-functions. Their leaders, together with picked S.A. men, were put into the posts of police-presidents. In April Himmler, the S.S. chief, was given charge under Göring of the Secret Police. In the same month a special body of Party police was formed, the *Feldjäger*, " to control the S.A., S.S., and Hitler Youth wherever they are removed from the direct supervision of their superiors ", as the official declaration ran. The position was ripe in June, under the barrage of the " Carpers and Grousers " campaign, for the government to open the attack.

It was announced that the S.A. would be given a holiday in July, and that Röhm would go on sick leave. Rumour had it that they would return from leave in a radically different form, and that Röhm was dismissed. Röhm countered by denying these rumours. It seems that he then attempted to organise a S.A. insurrection, throwing out feelers to Schleicher, the former chancellor, and Gregor Strasser, the former Nazi leader. The plans, ineffectual as they were, were discovered, and Hitler put a prompt end to them by executing the ringleaders, together with other persons who were better out of the way. There seems little doubt that Röhm's plans were not far advanced, and that the whole disaffection was more or less provoked by the government in order to deal a smashing blow at the S.A. The recent changes in the S.A. strengthen this view.

The S.S. has now been made independent of the S.A. Himmler holds the rank of S.S. Chief-of-Staff directly under Hitler. Lutze the new S.A. leader has no Ministerial post, and has already proclaimed far-reaching reforms of the S.A. Only members of the Nazi Party are henceforth to be allowed to be members of the S.A. The membership is to be sifted and all unreliable elements thrown out. A great number of leaders has been dismissed. The S.A. is to become an auxiliary police force, to be used against subversive activities, and has finally lost its revolutionary qualities. The illusions of 1932 and 1933 are gone.

What opposition can the disillusioned Storm Troopers, the disgruntled middle-class form, or join? In the National-Socialist State no moderate and modest opposition is possible. The dictatorship stretches into all branches of life and forbids the slightest censure of its actions. Opposition, if it is to exist, must be an absolute opposition. Amid all the grumbling in Germany to-day, there is only one Opposition—that of the revolutionary working-class, which aims at the overthrow of the capitalist dictatorship and the establishment of a Socialist Republic.

The tactics of the government with regard to the danger from the Communists vary. Some, like Göring, repeatedly draw attention to Communist activities, keeping the public alive to the necessity of violent repression, and threatening ever more draconic punishment. Others, like Goebbels, blandly declare that the Communists have disappeared from Germany, that their very name is forgotten. But there is a common policy of repression. Communist activities, when discovered, are rewarded by severe sentences of penal servitude. The government is aware that the menace of Communism is great, and greater since the S.A. has been emasculated.

Much of the news of Communist agitation in Germany is necessarily hard to verify. It is difficult to ascertain what strikes have taken place and how far they are definitely Communistic in origin; for strikes are of course now politically subversive and opposed by the whole force of the State. Books from Göring's department, like Sommerfeldt's *Kommune*, give a clearer indication of the extent of Communist agitation and the methods of Communist propaganda. The Communist campaign against Hitler's candidature for the Presidency was reported in all the foreign Press. Slogans are painted up all over Berlin, telephone directories are stamped with Anti-Nazi slogans. Above, all the reports from the Law Courts give a picture of Communist work.

Occasionally members of the Social-Democratic Party are punished for subversive activities—but very occasionally. More often groups of the Socialist Workers' Party are found distributing their leaflets. But these activities are overshadowed by the agitation of the Communist Party. A few Law Court reports of the last months show this. In May, 55 leaders of the Communist Party were sentenced in Mecklenburg. In June, 73 in Königsberg, 31 in Stettin, 3 in Hamburg, 12 in Breslau, 11 in Stralsund, 6 in Bremen. In July, 32 in Hamburg, 1 in Berlin,

5 in Saxony, 4 in Essen. At the beginning of August, on the very day on which Goebbels stated that Communism in Germany was forgotten, a Communist, Walter Duddins, was sentenced for having built in Hamburg a Party of 12,000 paying members. These figures, which are not complete, give a picture of widespread Communist activity which spells grave danger to the regime. Here is the centre of the Opposition to Hitler. This is the great danger to the rulers of Germany : that their former adherents, who have been so tricked and deceived, should be driven towards the Communists.

Which Way Out ?

How can the National-Socialist government escape from the economic, political, and social struggles in which it is involved ? Hitler cannot freely choose. Never was a Leader so bound in by hard necessity. He has fundamentally economic problems to solve, the problem of Unemployment and of low wages, the problem of national bankruptcy. The German ruling classes gave him Power in order to solve these problems ; he has done their work and is a willing tool in their hands.

The methods adopted have not been ambiguous. Germany is to find her prosperity in a complete system of Monopoly-Capitalism. The old chatter against the Trusts has been forgotten.[1] The old

[1] The official periodical, *Wirtschaft und Statistik*, writes (No. 4, 1934) : " In the period of 1933, the same tendencies have ruled as before : 1. Concentration of industry through the fusion of Joint-Stock Companies : 2. Elimination of small Companies."

Trusts have been strengthened, given State authority, cartellisation has penetrated into unheard-of corners. In the struggle for profit the most rigid capitalist organisation known to the world has been fashioned. Each industry, each branch of industry is governed by the big interests—firstly, through their power in the cartels, secondly by governmental authority, since the leaders of the industrial Groups and Sub-Groups all belong to the big concerns. The first aim of the big interests is to restrict production, to make competition impossible. Factories and shops are shut, quotas and prices fixed, so that profits are ensured. The class of wealth builds up around it impenetrable barriers of economic privilege. The abyss between the classes widens.

Under the stress of the political agitation of 1933, the State gave over five milliards of marks for work-schemes. To this alone is due the development of 1933–4. There is little enterprise to be marked in industry. The amount of new investment is very low, and far outweighed by the number of bankruptcies. Only in co-operative enterprise connected with agriculture has there been any development—in marketing-co-operatives for milk, etc., due to the new agricultural policy. National-Socialist "planning", so far as one can use the term, has consisted in restricting production so as to ensure that the State-subsidies turned into higher dividends. When the subsidies dry up, as is certain in the near future, it will be seen that there has been made no sound basis for the future. Further restriction will follow, with increasing impoverishment and misery. This will need still more rigid control. The process is already marked. The Minister for Trade, Schmitt, was made absolute dictator over Germany's economy ; when he, understandably, fell ill, Schacht took his place. Increasingly sharp measures are needed at the same time against social unrest. The Press is bullied into submission or liquidation. Radical opinion is hunted out.

Frozen in its monopolies, German capitalism sees only one way out of its economic and social impasse —a war. Only by winning colonies, where it can find its raw materials and also a market for its goods, does the government believe it can be delivered. Thus all the " reforms " in Germany to-day serve, directly or indirectly, the cause of militarism. Her industries take rank of preference in proportion as they are militarily valuable. It is the common talk among the German middle-classes, that Germany must fight. Without the promise and hope of a war, the German government stands for nothing but further repression and impoverishment. War is certain and feverishly prepared for.

The main force in Germany to-day is Monopoly-Capitalism. Its policy is war. It is not necessary, then, that the government should remain in its present form. There is no absolute need for a " gangster " dictatorship to prevail. Precisely those forces which brought Hitler to power, the big industrial and agricultural interests who achieved, in January 1933, the compromise between Von Papen and Hitler, may find it necessary to govern through different men. All institutions through which their working-class opponents may work have been destroyed. A law and society has been created which will allow of the maximum of legal oppression. Thus concessions to " decent ", conservative opinion may be expected. Already signs of this have appeared. Von Papen's speech at Marburg in June was a first open demand for a return to normal, ordered government. The Social-Democratic Saar newspaper, *Deutsche Freiheit*, notes with some satisfaction the appearance of an illegal leaflet in Berlin appealing for a common front of " decent " opinion. Most significantly of all, the *Manchester Guardian* of August 7 reports discussions between representatives of Hitler and Social-Democracy. The latter, above all the old Trade Union bureaucracy, are, according to the report, to be utilised in organising the Labour Front, in establishing contact between the government and the working-class. Social-Democracy, which supported Brüning and Hindenburg against Hitler, is to go one farther on its way and support " decent " dictatorship against " gangster " dictatorship.

These possibilities remain open for the future. But there is no possibility, within the present framework of German society, to reintroduce any of the institutions of democracy. Never again can German capitalism allow the working-class the right of organisation. If the German masses—and here the lower middle-class is included—are to gain freedom again, there is only one way for them. This way is directly opposed to the whole organisation of Hitler-Germany. It is the way of Socialism, the overthrow of decent as well as gangster Dictatorship. This solution does not seem near. Power is entirely in the hands of the rulers. But the movement of the masses is unmistakable. We should not be misled by monster demonstrations and votes. The lower middle-class in particular is characterised by political instability. But it is already confused and dismayed, if not antagonised, by the antics of its demagogic leaders. Little is needed to swing it over into active opposition. Not opinion stands in the way of the social Revolution, but Power. And, as Goebbels himself said when in Opposition, a government cannot indefinitely rule by bayonets.

INDEX

INDEX

INDEX

INDEX

INDEX

INDEX

INDEX